Clean Eating Kitchen

THE LOW-CARB
MEDITERRANEAN
COOKBOOK

Clean Eating Kitchen

THE LOW-CARB MEDITERRANEAN COOKBOOK

Quick and Easy High-Protein,
Low-Sugar, Healthy-Fat Recipes
for Lifelong Health

MICHELLE DUDASH, R.D.N.,

Author of *Clean Eating for Busy Families*

FAIR WINDS

Brimming with creative inspiration, how-to projects, and useful information to enrich your everyday life, Quarto Knows is a favorite destination for those pursuing their interests and passions. Visit our site and dig deeper with our books into your area of interest: Quarto Creates, Quarto Cooks, Quarto Homes, Quarto Lives, Quarto Drives, Quarto Explores, Quarto Gifts, or Quarto Kids.

First Published in 2021 by Fair Winds Press, an imprint of The Quarto Group, 100 Cummings Center, Suite 265-D, Beverly, MA 01915, USA.
T (978) 282-9590 F (978) 283-2742 QuartoKnows.com

Fair Winds Press titles are also available at discount for retail, wholesale, promotional, and bulk purchase. For details, contact the Special Sales Manager by email at specialsales@quarto.com or by mail at The Quarto Group, Attn: Special Sales Manager, 100 Cummings Center, Suite 265-D, Beverly, MA 01915, USA.

25 24 23 22 21   2 3 4 5

ISBN: 978-1-59233-988-4

Digital edition published in 2021

Library of Congress Cataloging-in-Publication Data available.

Design: The Quarto Group
Cover Image: Jo Harding Photography
Page Layout: *tabula rasa* graphic design
Photography and styling: Jo Harding www.modernfoodstories.com

Printed in China

The information in this book is for educational purposes only. It is not intended to replace the advice of a physician or medical practitioner. Please see your health-care provider before beginning any new health program.

Dedication

For Steve, who is always game for an adventure across the pond with me.

To Scarlet and Stella, I cherish every meal we share around the table.

Contents

Introduction
Why I Wrote This Book for You

Through my years of working as a cookbook author, dietitian, recipe and product developer, television personality, private and personal chef, caterer, and food writer, I've observed one constant: the majority of adults reach for protein foods the most and starchy foods the least. (Okay, except French fries.)

This is in line with the many people I have talked with about their eating habits. From surgeons to stay-at-home moms to hair stylists to sales executives, they strive to build the bulk of their plate with protein foods and non-starchy vegetables. These people report feeling their best when on a low-carb eating regimen. As a registered dietitian and nutritionist for twenty years, I have discovered that there is not one perfect eating plan that works for everyone's DNA, culture, budget, lifestyle, and metabolism. I encourage people to find the eating style that they can stick to and enjoy for the long term that makes them feel good, both mentally and physically, while keeping chronic disease and inflammation at bay.

Despite good intentions, however, I see smart people dependent on highly processed, fatty meats and cheese to reach daily protein goals while in pursuit of a smaller waistline and blood sugar control. The problem is that people who eat more of these foods may then be putting themselves at an increased risk for high cholesterol, heart disease, stroke, cancer, and digestive issues, to name a few. Luckily, there is a better to go about this. You can achieve results by following the top eating pattern ranked year after year by credentialed medical professionals: the Mediterranean diet. However, this can be improved even further by tapering back on refined grains and sugar, an alternative plan known as the low-carb Mediterranean diet.

These factors, in addition to eating my way through numerous Mediterranean countries, inspired me to write this book for you, combining the beautiful, nourishing food of this region, while scaling back on carbs to adapt to modern-day eating preferences.

Bon appétit. Buon appetito. Buen provecho.
Chef Michelle Dudash, R.D.N.

1

Low-Carb Mediterranean Know-How:
What It Is, Who It's for, and How to Make It Work for You

Enjoying low-carb recipes doesn't have to be an all-the-time or all-or-nothing proposition. This chapter details how to fit low-carb recipes into your routine and in a way that works for your lifestyle.

My Mediterranean Background

It all began for me in the kitchen, of course. My Lebanese grandmother and *her* mother introduced me to the foods of their native country. There was always amazing, home-made food at the ready upon walking into either of their kitchens. They were the OGs of meal prep! From mostly parsley tabbouleh to lettuce salad with fresh lemon-mint vinaigrette to stuffed grape leaves, you would have never guessed I was growing up in a town of 36,000 people in the state of Wisconsin in the 1980s. (Shout-out to my hometown of Fond du Lac, Wisconsin, and also home to a group of Lebanese immigrants.)

After earning degrees and certifications as a registered dietitian nutritionist and Le Cordon Bleu chef in my early twenties, my next goal was to travel. Over the years, with my husband or colleagues, I have sought out various Mediterranean cities, towns, and countrysides spanning Italy, France, Monaco, Spain, and Croatia, with a top goal of devouring everything in sight, trying new foods to educate my palate. I enrolled in cooking classes in these countries, visited food production plants, and toured food markets. I sipped my way through some wineries, too. My travels have certainly influenced how I build my plate, grocery shop, cook, entertain, and feed my family. And I still have many Mediterranean countries left to visit, like Greece, Turkey, Israel, and more!

About the Mediterranean Diet

Originally introduced in 1993 by the Harvard School of Public Health, the Oldways Preservation and Exchange Trust, and the European Office of the World Health Organization, the Mediterranean diet went on to be added to the USDA's *Dietary Guidelines for Americans 2015–2020* as a recommended meal plan option, brushing elbows with MyPlate, the modern version of the Food Guide Pyramid. This was a pretty big deal because when the government endorses something, you know it has gone through many hoops and levels of approval and scrutiny to earn that spot. Medical professionals, including registered dietitians, love the Mediterranean diet, too. The *U.S. News & World Report* has ranked the Mediterranean diet as Best Diet Overall in 2020 (third year in a row), second in Best Heart-Healthy Diet, first in Best Diabetes Diet, first in Best Diet for Healthy Eating, and first in Easiest Diet to Follow.

Grains, vegetables, and fruits lie at the foundation of the traditional Mediterranean Food Pyramid; however, the reality is that a lot of us are trying to avoid excessive amounts of starchy foods like pasta, rice, and bread in order to lose weight, control blood sugar levels for diabetes management or prevention, feel less bloated, and feel better in general. The good news is that you can still enjoy some grains, especially the whole-food versions, in moderation. It needn't be the center of the plate.

The low-carb Mediterranean diet delivers the best of both worlds, satisfying a mostly plant- and seafood-based regimen that is higher in protein and heart-healthy fats while being lower in carbs, but focusing on high-quality carbs. This book combines the healthiest and most crave-worthy ingredients and flavors of the Mediterranean diet that are sure to induce wanderlust, including vegetables and fruits, herbs and spices, some legumes, extra-virgin olive oil, nuts and seeds, seafood, some dairy and poultry, a bit of red meat, and some whole grains here and there.

Low-Carb 101

There are three main categories of macronutrients and how we get our calories, or energy: carbohydrates, protein, and fat. Plus, alcohol, for people who consume it. Vitamins and minerals are micronutrients; while they don't provide calories, they help us with all sorts of processes carried out by the body.

Within the carb category, there are different types, many of which you even see called out on food labels. These carbs generally contain 4 calories per gram:

Complex carbohydrates are long chains of molecules that take the body some time to break down, giving you a steadier stream of energy. *Found in: potatoes, rice, and pasta.*

Fiber, a component only naturally found in plants, is made up of two types: soluble and insoluble. Fiber is important for regulating digestion and can help lower cholesterol and blood sugar.

Soluble fiber is dissolvable in liquid, and the body absorbs half of these carbs. *Found in: oats (the soluble fiber makes oats gel as they cool), blueberries, and the white pulp of apples.*

Insoluble fiber, on the other hand, does not dissolve in water. If you added ground-up insoluble fiber to a glass of water, it would eventually settle to the bottom. This fiber is not absorbed by the body, and therefore does not actually provide the body with calories, but it acts as a natural broom for the digestive system. *Found in: green beans, apple skin, and brown rice.*

Sugar, also a type of carbohydrate, contributes the same 4 calories per gram as complex carbs; however, it can be absorbed very quickly by the body when in foods devoid of fiber, fat, or protein. The body handles these sugar molecules in pretty much the same way, and at the end of the day, all sugars are broken down into fructose (fruit sugar), galactose (part of lactose, the milk sugar), or glucose, a preferred energy source for the brain and muscles. Sugar can be found in foods as added sugar or naturally occurring sugar.

Added sugars include white cane or beet sugar, brown rice syrup, agave nectar, brown sugar, and evaporated cane juice, which are virtually void of other nutrients. Two added sugars with fringe benefits include honey (potential antibacterial properties when fresh) and molasses (variety of vitamins and minerals). Caloric soda beverages and hard candies are made of pure added sugar, in general, and are devoid of fiber, fat, and protein.

Naturally occurring sugars are found in fruits and some vegetables, animal milk–based drinks and yogurt, and 100 percent fruit juices. All of these foods are rich in a variety of beneficial nutrients.

The Various Levels of Low-Carb Diets

Keeping an eye on your carb intake doesn't have to mean going all-or-nothing. While there isn't a standard clinical definition of what is considered a "low-carb diet," medical experts have attempted to define "low-carb" to lessen the confusion for medical professionals and patients with diabetes. Here is one, as defined by Richard D. Feinman, Ph.D., a professor of cell biology at the State University of New

York Downstate Medical Center, where he and colleagues reviewed a number of studies on carbohydrate levels:

Very low-carbohydrate ketogenic diet: A range of 30 to 50 grams of carbohydrates per day, or less than 10 percent of total calories consumed*

Low-carbohydrate diet: Fewer than 130 grams per day, or less than 26 percent of total calories consumed*

Moderate-carbohydrate diet: Greater than 130 grams per day, or 26 to 45 percent of total calories consumed*

Based on a 2,000-calorie diet.

Traditional Mediterranean diets fit into the moderate-carbohydrate diet level. Since there are a number of Mediterranean countries with different cuisines and foods, the amounts can vary. For example, one study of the Greek Mediterranean diet found 41 percent calories from carbohydrates, 40 percent from fat, and 19 percent from protein. A study looking at diets in Southern Italy revealed 58 percent calories from carbohydrates, while averaging 31 grams fiber per day. In the ANIBES study, Spanish adults revealed a diet comprised of 40 percent carbohydrates.

For those who wish to reap the benefits of the Mediterranean diet while still cutting back on carbs, some fine tweaks can be made. The low-carbohydrate diet of fewer than 130 grams of carbs per day still allows for some whole grains, legumes, and fruits. The very low-carbohydrate ketogenic diet has little room for grains and legumes, with some lower-carb fruits, like berries, still fitting into the mix.

It's important to note that a daily low-carb diet distribution is not recommended for children and pregnant and breastfeeding women, plus most sports nutritionists advise against a low-carb diet for athletes due to decreased performance over time. The low carb recipes in this book, however, can be enjoyed by almost everyone, since it is the sum of meals and snacks and drinks throughout the day that add up to total nutrition.

The Staple Ingredients of the Low-Carb Mediterranean Diet
Extra-Virgin Olive Oil
Buy quarterly, enjoy at most meals

With heart-healthy monounsaturated and polyunsaturated fats making up a large percentage of fat in the Mediterranean diet, it's important to point out that extra-virgin olive oil is the staple fat used in cooking and at the table, from sautéing seafood to drizzling over salads and cooked vegetables—even stirring into cake batter! While vacationing in Spain, I learned to love drizzling olive oil on my breakfast toast instead of using butter or margarine. Keep in mind that ounce for ounce, olive oil is *higher* in calories and fat compared to butter, but it is lower in saturated fat and contains no cholesterol. It's the heart-healthy fat in olive oil that is largely responsible for its health benefits.

This greenish golden oil is highest in monounsaturated fat, compared to other fats, and is rich in polyphenols, the anti-inflammatory compounds that help fight disease. Extra-virgin olive oil comes from the first "pressing," although there isn't actually a press anymore. Instead, the crushed olives are put through a spinning technique, called centrifugation. Don't fall for oils labeled as "pure olive oil" or "light olive oil," as these oils are the result of chemical extraction from the olives, making them the sloppy seconds, thus lacking in the beneficial polyphenols. I buy olive oil by the gallon (3.8 L) (for a family of four) and decant it into an opaque bottle with a narrow pour spout for easy access. This saves money, too. Store oils away from heat and light to prolong shelf life. Unopened olive oil can last one-and-a-half to two years, while opened bottles only last in the range of months, depending on how carefully you store it. If it smells bad, it's gone bad, so throw it out.

Vegetables, Beans, and Legumes
Buy daily or weekly, enjoy at all or most meals

A wide range of colorful (and white, too!) vegetables should make up about one-third to one-half of the plate. Different colored produce each represent different disease-fighting compounds. Eat the vegetables you enjoy that are in season and abundant, which will probably taste better, be higher in nutrients, and save you money compared to out-of-season produce available in limited quantities.

When following a low-carb regimen, you'll want to load up on non-starchy vegetables like broccoli, cucumbers, lettuce, Brussels sprouts, tomatoes (although technically a fruit), and asparagus. Starchy vegetables like potatoes, corn, and peas contribute more carbs, but also fiber, so if you love these foods, you can still incorporate them in smart ways. Fresh, frozen, and canned vegetables all count, so use what works for your budget, lifestyle, and taste preferences; I use all three.

Fruits
Buy daily or weekly, enjoy a few times per day

Fruits can fit when eating low-carb, since they are high in fiber and rich in nutrients. A big bowl of fruit typically ends the meal in Mediterranean countries, with traditional sweetened desserts reserved for perhaps just a few times per week and on special occasions. Reach for mostly fresh or frozen, which have a higher water content, to help keep you satisfied longer. When eating dried fruit, choose those with no added sugar. Canned fruits are better than nothing, but usually have the fibrous skins removed and may be soaked in syrup.

Nuts and Seeds
Buy weekly or monthly, enjoy at least once per day

A serving a day may keep the doctor away! Nuts and seeds contribute plant-based protein, potassium, fiber, and more. Nuts and seeds needn't be reserved just for snack time, either, although I do love them as a grab-and-go afternoon snack. I often sprinkle them into yogurt or over salads, spread a nut butter on toast or use as a fruit or vegetable dip, or even puree them into dips, dressings, or sauces.

Herbs and Spices
Buy as needed, enjoy at all meals

As a chef, I absolutely relish adding herbs and spices to my recipes, since they can completely turn a few simple ingredients like a protein or a vegetable into a flavorful entrée with depth. But you may be like a lot of people I talk to, who are confused as to which herb or spice goes with which food! Not to worry. In this book, I walk you through the exact herbs and spices to use in each recipe to make the dish sing. After you're through, you'll have built up a nice little arsenal of natural flavorings to add to dishes, even when you're cooking from the hip. Also check out my Dash Dinners™ Spice Kits at dashdinners. com for more recipe inspiration. You will find complete seasoning blends in convenient packets for quick family meals.

Seafood
Buy daily or weekly, enjoy at least twice per week

Enjoying seafood at least twice a week is recommended across even the USDA's *Dietary Guidelines*; however, Americans are eating less than half that amount. Seafood is a source of omega-3 fatty acids DHA and EPA, types of polyunsaturated fats that have been found to be good for the heart and brain, and overall for anti-inflammatory effects. These omega-3 fatty acids vary in different seafood species, in general, aim for a variety. From fresh to frozen to canned seafood, all are nutritious and all count. Eat those that fit your budget, are available at your grocer, and that you like best.

Poultry and Eggs
Buy weekly, enjoy a few times per week, up to daily

Chicken, turkey, and other fowl can be enjoyed a few times per week up to daily. If your comfort zone usually equates to chicken breast, I am here to assure you that many other delicious, lean proteins await!

If you love your eggs in the morning, you'll be glad to know that the Mediterranean diet includes up to seven eggs per week.

Dairy
Buy weekly, enjoy a few times per week, up to daily

Yogurt and cheese fit in the Mediterranean diet, if you wish, but in smaller amounts, including a few times per week, up to daily. This is a drastic contrast compared to the three servings a day you were raised hearing about. While dairy provides a variety of essential nutrients like calcium, you can also get these from plant-based foods if you are eating a balanced diet.

Milk is fortified with vitamin D, as are more and more foods these days. Considering that many people are falling short in vitamin D, putting their bone health at risk, sun exposure on legs and arms twice weekly for 20 minutes at a time will help your body make vitamin D. This amount of sun isn't easy for everyone to get, especially depending on where you live. Taking a vitamin D3 supplement after consulting with your medical professional will solve that problem.

Red Meat
Buy and enjoy weekly, if you wish

As to how much red meat you can eat on the Mediterranean diet, there are a few things to consider in deciding what may work best for you.

The Oldways version of the Mediterranean diet recommends eating red meat, which includes beef, pork, and lamb, up to a total of 12 to 16 ounces (340 to 454 g) per month. This equates to a portion the size of a deck of cards three or four times a month. But all red meat is not equal. If you are choosing mostly lean and unprocessed meat, you may be able to enjoy more meat healthfully. (Unprocessed meat includes fresh or frozen meat that hasn't been cured or smoked, unlike bacon and sausage, which are.)

Studies examining actual dietary patterns of people *living* in the Mediterranean reveal diets containing a bit more meat. For example, in a study examining the diets of about 1,800 Southern Italian adults, the average daily intake of unprocessed meats was about 1 ounce (28 g) per day and about ½ ounce (14 g) per day of processed meat, though these Italians rely more on high-quality cured meats instead of fast food. This group also averaged 1 ounce (28 g) of beans and legumes per day, getting nearly twice as many calories per day from plant protein versus animal protein. The take-home message? Eat a variety of protein sources.

It's okay to eat unprocessed, lean red meat once or twice a week if you enjoy it.

Ideally, select lean unprocessed cuts, like the ones I use in this book, which are lower in saturated fat and cholesterol compared to fattier cuts. If your portion is about the size of a deck of cards, or 4 ounces (112 g), you can enjoy a serving once or twice per week. If you prefer to not eat meat, replace it with different protein sources like poultry, seafood, eggs, nuts and seeds, and legumes.

Sweets
Enjoy a few times per week, if you wish

Yes, sweetened desserts may light up your pleasure centers in the short term, but their high content of added and refined sugars, butter, and refined flours can wreak havoc on your health over time, putting them at the tippy-top of the Mediterranean Food Pyramid—meaning to eat as little as possible. It's more beneficial to satisfy your sweet tooth with some luscious, fresh, in-season fruit. Or maybe even dip it into some melted dark chocolate—a favorite pastime with my daughters. This isn't to say you can *never* enjoy sweets. Just do so wisely.

Whenever we visit restaurants in Italy, I notice large platters of fresh, lush fruit brought out to the table at the end of the meal, with a big steak knife stuck into it. This is a good practice to get into, rather than always relying on sweetened desserts. In this book, I included a dessert chapter for those of you who *need* it. I use real sugar because I'd rather have a small amount of the real thing just occasionally than artificial sweeteners more often. I aim to load up on protein-rich almond flour, which is also low-carb, instead of wheat flour, and am generous with nuts and seeds, fruit, dark chocolate, and spices for flavor.

When you're away from home and surrounded by traditional sweets and can't resist the temptation, try just taking a few bites of something really good, or share the dessert with friends.

Did Someone Say Wine?

The Mediterranean diet includes wine—that's right! Up to one 5-ounce (140 ml) glass per day for women, and up to two 5-ounce (140 ml) glasses per day for men. There is something magical about the polyphenols in wine, and researchers are discovering that any type of alcohol, really, has a beneficial effect on a variety of organ systems in the body. More than the recommended daily amount, however, has a negative effect.

That's not to say that everyone should drink wine, however. Current guidelines recommend that pregnant women, alcoholics, and people with liver disease abstain from alcohol. If you don't currently drink, it is probably better to just keep it that way. One hundred percent Concord grape juice is also rich in polyphenols, making it another nutritious alternative.

In terms of carbs, dry wines are lowest, with 5 to 6 grams of carbs per 5-ounce (140 ml) serving.

How to Use Net Carbs in This Book

Net carbs are a handy little tool to have for people counting carbs. Net carbs are calculated as follows:

Total Carbs – Dietary Fiber = Net Carbs

You can use this calculation because most fiber is not digested, and therefore does not provide calories or affect blood sugar. The body does not absorb any insoluble fiber. About half of the calories from soluble fiber are absorbed, they are first fermented in the intestine but then broken down into fatty acids, therefore having negligible effect, if any, on blood sugar.

In this book, I have included net carb values with every recipe for your convenience.

Tips for Getting Started

My best advice for starting any dietary change is to just start! You can begin by making even just one of these meals each week. Little by little, you can make healthy swaps, with simple changes in your daily habits adding up to big results over time. Here are more tips:

- You don't have to go all in, go "cold turkey," or give up all the foods you love. It's about balance over time. Here are more tips:

- Listen to your body. Eat when you are truly hungry. Don't eat when you're not hungry.

- Feed the beast. Some days you may feel that you need more carbs, and that is completely okay. Factors like grueling workouts and hormonal fluctuations can affect metabolic needs.

- If you don't like it, change it. If you hate eating raw veggie sticks, then don't! There are so many delicious foods out there and available. Eat what you enjoy that fits into your plan.

- Shed the guilt. If you choose to eat something that isn't on your plan, acknowledge why you did it and move on. Beating yourself up about it will get you nowhere, damaging your relationship with food. And there's no such thing as "good" or "bad" foods. Some are healthier and some are less so. Strive to choose more of the healthful ones, and leave it at that.

- Ease in on the high-fiber foods. It really does take time for your body to adjust to a high-fiber diet to avoid any unpleasantries like gas and bloating. The bacteria in your gut need time to ramp up gradually to handle the load.

- If you are on diabetes medication, always check with your doctor or dietitian first before making changes to your carbohydrate intake.

- A low-carb diet is not suitable for children, pregnant women, and breastfeeding women. These groups can enjoy the recipes in this book, but add in some fruits, whole grains, and starchy vegetables for some healthful carbs.

- Perhaps most importantly, enjoy every bite! Life is short. Eat flavorful food that energizes you, brings you joy, and gives you vitality, inside and out.

30 Minutes or Less
The clock icon listed at the bottom of many of the recipes in this book designates that the recipe can be prepared in 30 minutes or less.

2

Lively Starters: Appetizers, Salads, Snacks, Soups, and Sips

Discover a whole world of delicious low-carb snacks and starter courses, packed with protein, nuts, seeds, vegetables, and cheese. Enjoy.

DEVILED EGGS WITH BASIL AND PINE NUTS

There are so many flavorful ways you can prepare deviled eggs. From my experience as a chef, they are a hit at every party, making them versatile for brunches, lunches, snacks, and appetizers. If you want to be really efficient, double the pesto ingredients and remove half before you add the eggs, so you have freshly made pesto for other uses, like zoodles and dips.

1 dozen large eggs

½ teaspoon salt, divided

1 clove garlic, peeled

¼ cup (34 g) pine nuts (or walnuts)

2 cups (80 g) fresh basil leaves, lightly packed, plus tiny basil leaves for garnishing

¼ cup (25 g) grated Parmesan

1 tablespoon (15 ml) lemon juice

Freshly ground black pepper

¼ cup (60 ml) extra-virgin olive oil

Place the eggs in a pot and cover with water. Bring to a low boil over high heat. Reduce the heat as needed to maintain a low boil for 12 minutes. Remove the eggs from the heat and carefully drain the pot. Fill the pot with cold water and a handful of ice to cool the eggs quickly. Peel the eggs and slice them in half lengthwise. Gently remove the yolks. Arrange the egg whites on a baking sheet lined with a paper towel. Sprinkle the whites with ¼ teaspoon of the salt.

Add the garlic and pine nuts to a food processor to chop finely. Add the basil and process until chopped finely. Add the Parmesan, lemon juice, remaining ¼ teaspoon salt, and pepper and pulse a few times to mix. While running the food processor, slowly drizzle in the oil. (If you made a double batch of pesto for other uses, now is the time to take out half.)

Add the yolks to the food processor and process until smooth.

Spoon the mix into a small resealable plastic bag and cut ¼ inch (6 mm) from a bottom corner, or use a piping bag with a tip. Twist the bag to push all of the filling toward the tip and squeeze to fill the egg whites with the yolk mixture.

Cover lightly and chill until ready to serve, up to 4 days.

Recipe Note

Use older eggs for deviled eggs when possible, because they are easier to peel than fresher eggs. Older eggs have lost some moisture content, creating air gaps between the egg sac and the shell, helping release the shell more easily.

TOTAL PREP AND COOK TIME: 1 HOUR · YIELD: 24 SERVINGS, ½ EGG EACH

PER SERVING: 64 CALORIES, 0 G CARBOHYDRATE (0 G FIBER, 0 G ADDED SUGARS, 0 G NET CARBS), 4 G PROTEIN, 5 G FAT, 96 MG SODIUM.

ROASTED CAULIFLOWER HUMMUS

Hummus lovers: Here's another rendition that will really surprise your taste buds.

4 cups (400 g) cauliflower florets

2 cloves garlic, with skin on

2 tablespoons (30 ml) extra-virgin olive oil, plus more for drizzling

¼ teaspoon ground cumin

¼ teaspoon ground turmeric

¼ teaspoon salt

Freshly ground black pepper

1 tablespoon (15 g) tahini

1 tablespoon (15 ml) lime juice

2 tablespoons (16 g) toasted pine nuts or sliced almonds

Coarsely chopped cilantro (optional)

Preheat the oven to 425°F (220°C, or gas mark 7) convection. Line a baking sheet with parchment paper or a silicone baking mat.

Place the cauliflower and garlic on the prepared baking sheet. Drizzle the cauliflower with the oil. Sprinkle with the cumin, turmeric, salt, and pepper. Roast until the cauliflower is fork tender, 15 to 20 minutes. Reserve some of the tiny cauliflower bits for the garnish, if you'd like, and if you can resist eating them immediately. Squeeze the garlic cloves out of their skins.

Place the cauliflower, garlic, tahini, and lime juice in a food processor and puree until smooth. To serve, spread in a wide, shallow dish. Drizzle with olive oil and sprinkle with the pine nuts and cilantro, if using.

TOTAL PREP AND COOK TIME: 30 MINUTES · YIELD: 8 SERVINGS, 2 TABLESPOONS (32 G) EACH

<30 PER SERVING: 77 CALORIES, 4 G CARBOHYDRATE (1 G FIBER, 0 G ADDED SUGARS, 3 G NET CARBS), 2 G PROTEIN, 7 G FAT, 91 MG SODIUM.

TAHINI-ZUCCHINI DIP

If you're all "hummused out" and want to wake up your taste buds, give this dip a try. The base of this dip is tahini, which is made of ground sesame seeds, plus zucchini to lighten it up a bit while adding a pop of color. I love dipping crispy sliced radishes or carrots into this, or serving it as a dip with chicken.

1 clove garlic, peeled

1 medium zucchini, sliced

½ cup (130 g) tahini (sesame seed paste; see Recipe Note)

¼ cup (60 ml) lemon juice

½ teaspoon salt

In a food processor, mince the garlic. Add the zucchini and process until finely chopped. Add the tahini, lemon juice, and salt. Process until smooth.

Suggestions and Variations
Sprinkle ground sumac, a spice, on top for an added pop of color and intense lemony taste.

Recipe Note
At grocery stores, you can find tahini in jars in the nut butter section or in cans in the international food section.

TOTAL PREP AND COOK TIME: 20 MINUTES · YIELD: 8 SERVINGS, ¼ CUP (65 G) EACH

PER SERVING: 94 CALORIES, 4 G CARBOHYDRATE (1 G FIBER, 0 G ADDED SUGARS, 3 G NET CARBS), 3 G PROTEIN, 8 G FAT, 152 MG SODIUM.

CREAMY SPINACH PIE WITH ALMOND FLOUR CRUST

If you love the flavors of spanakopita, a Greek appetizer traditionally layered with phyllo dough, then you'll love this dish. Here, I swap the phyllo with an almond flour crust, eliminating refined carbs and additional time required to make the layers. You just get pure protein, nuts, veggies, and deliciousness!

You can enjoy this as an appetizer cut into squares or have a larger square for breakfast or lunch.

FOR THE CRUST:

Cooking oil spray

1 tablespoon + 2 teaspoons (13 g) flaxseed meal

3 tablespoons (45 ml) water

1 cup (96 g) almond flour or meal

½ teaspoon dried oregano

⅛ teaspoon salt

Freshly ground black pepper

1 tablespoon (15 ml) extra-virgin olive oil

FOR THE FILLING:

1 tablespoon (15 ml) extra-virgin olive oil

½ medium onion, finely chopped (about 1 cup [160 g])

2 cloves garlic, minced

1 bag (10-ounce [280 g]) spinach

5 ounces (140 g) soft goat cheese, sliced

½ teaspoon dried oregano

¼ teaspoon salt

Freshly ground black pepper

2 large eggs

¼ cup (27 g) sliced almonds

To make the crust: Preheat the oven to 350°F (180°C, or gas mark 4). Coat a 9 × 9-inch (23 × 23 cm) baking dish with oil spray. In a medium bowl, combine the flaxseed and water. Add the almond flour, oregano, salt, and pepper, and stir with a fork. Drizzle in the oil and stir until it forms a dough. Spoon the dough into the baking dish, spreading into an even layer, with dough going about ¼ inch (6 mm) up the sides of the dish, and press gently with your fingers to form a crust. Bake on the middle rack until light golden, about 18 minutes.

To make the filling: Place a large pot over medium heat. Add the oil. When the oil is hot, add the onion and garlic, reduce the heat to medium-low, and gently sauté until the onions are translucent, about 5 minutes. Add the spinach and toss continuously until most of it is wilted, about 2 minutes. Remove from the heat. Stir in the goat cheese, oregano, salt, and pepper. Stir in the eggs. Spoon the filling into the crust and sprinkle with the almonds. Bake until the center is firm and the almonds are golden around the edges, about 28 minutes.

TOTAL PREP AND COOK TIME: 1 HOUR · YIELD: 16 SERVINGS, 1 SQUARE EACH

PER SERVING: 113 CALORIES, 3 G CARBOHYDRATE (2 G FIBER, 0 G ADDED SUGARS, 1 G NET CARBS), 5 G PROTEIN, 9 G FAT, 122 MG SODIUM.

GREEK 7-LAYER HUMMUS DIP

I served this to my gaggle of girlfriends for a pre-dinner wine and snack meet-up during an active tennis vacation and it was so easy to throw together while feeling oh-so Mediterranean, fresh, healthy, and light. 1 pan + 9 women = gone.

Serve with your favorite dipping vessels, like red bell pepper planks, celery sticks, and sliced zucchini.

1 container (8-ounce [227 g]) hummus,* like classic, roasted red pepper, or lemon flavor (see Suggestions and Variations)

1 medium cucumber, peeled and diced (leave the seeds in if they are small)

1 cup (150 g) sliced cherry tomatoes

3 scallions, sliced

½ cup (75 g) crumbled feta cheese

¼ cup (25 g) sliced olives, such as kalamata

1 teaspoon dried oregano or Italian seasoning

Freshly ground black pepper

2 tablespoons (30 ml) extra-virgin olive oil

Spread the hummus in the bottom of a 9 × 9-inch (23 × 23 cm) glass dish or similar-size platter. Sprinkle with the cucumber, tomatoes, scallions, feta, olives, oregano, and pepper. Drizzle with the oil.

Suggestions and Variations

If you prefer this dip *completely* homemade, make my Tahini-Zucchini Dip on page 21, instead of using store-bought hummus.

Make It for the Whole Family
* My young daughters, who are relatively selective eaters, just *love* hummus, but prefer it plain. If you think that may be the case for your kids, be sure to buy the super-size tub of hummus and reserve some for them. Serve with their favorite raw veggie sticks.

TOTAL PREP AND COOK TIME: 30 MINUTES · YIELD: 16 SERVINGS, ABOUT ¼ CUP (60 G) EACH

PER SERVING: 59 CALORIES, 4 G CARBOHYDRATE (1 G FIBER, 0 G ADDED SUGARS, 3 G NET CARBS), 2 G PROTEIN, 4 G FAT, 104 MG SODIUM.

RED PEPPERY WALNUT-HERB DIP (MUHAMMARA)

This dip is a take on *muhammara*, a colorful red dip originating from Syria, made of a base of roasted red peppers and walnuts. Bread crumbs are traditionally used, but instead I just amped up the amount of walnuts. I toast the walnuts too, giving the dip a nuttier, more intense flavor. You can use this as a dip with raw vegetables like cauliflower florets or almond flour crackers, or use it to brighten up grilled chicken or fish. I took a few liberties in this recipe, too, swapping out a couple of specialty-store ingredients, like pomegranate molasses and Aleppo chiles.

2 medium red bell peppers

2 tablespoons (30 ml) extra-virgin olive oil, plus extra for rubbing and drizzling

¾ cup (90 g) walnut halves, plus extra for garnish

1 clove garlic, peeled

1 teaspoon chili powder,* plus extra for garnish

1 teaspoon balsamic vinegar

¼ teaspoon salt

Freshly ground black pepper

Move an oven rack to 6 inches (15 cm) below the broiler and another oven rack to the middle of the oven. Preheat the oven to low broil. Line two baking sheets with parchment paper.

Place the peppers on one of the prepared baking sheets and rub with some oil. Place on the top rack. Place the walnuts on the other prepared baking sheet in a single layer and place on the middle rack. Set a timer for 5 minutes for the walnuts and remove from the oven when they smell toasted, but before they get too brown. Roast the peppers until blistered all over, about 15 minutes, turning as needed.

When the peppers are blistered all over, remove from the oven and place in a bag and seal, allowing them to cool to the point where you can handle them, about 5 minutes. Peel and core the peppers. Cut into a few chunks.

In a food processor, finely chop the garlic. Add the roasted peppers, walnuts, 2 tablespoons (30 ml) oil, chili powder, balsamic, salt, and pepper. Pulse until mostly smooth.

Place in a shallow bowl or on a platter, making a well in the center. Sprinkle with some broken-up walnuts, a sprinkle of chili powder, and drizzle with oil.

Suggestions and Variations
* If you'd like to kick up the heat, add 1/4 teaspoon crushed red pepper flakes.

TOTAL PREP AND COOK TIME: 40 MINUTES · YIELD: 8 SERVINGS, 2 TABLESPOONS (30 G) EACH

PER SERVING: 40 CALORIES, 3 G CARBOHYDRATE (0 G FIBER, 0 G ADDED SUGARS, 3 G NET CARBS), 0 G PROTEIN, 3 G FAT, 74 MG SODIUM.

ITALIAN-INSPIRED GUACAMOLE WITH BALSAMIC, RED ONION, AND BASIL

I'm guacamole- and avocado-obsessed like you, most likely. So why not create a guacamole with an Italian twist? Balsamic is an awesome pairing with avocados. A favorite snack of mine during prime-time avocado season is to mash avocado on a cracker and spritz it with balsamic vinegar.

3 large, ripe avocados

1 large tomato, diced, divided

¼ cup (140 g) diced red onion

¼ cup (10 g) chiffonade basil (stack leaves, roll, and slice thinly)

1 tablespoon (15 ml) balsamic vinegar

½ teaspoon salt

¼ teaspoon crushed red pepper flakes

⅛ teaspoon garlic powder

Freshly ground black pepper

2 tablespoons (16 g) toasted pine nuts or chopped almonds

Peel and pit the avocados, saving the pits. Mash the avocados in a medium bowl using the sides of 2 large spoons. Stir in half of the tomatoes*, onion, basil, balsamic, salt, red pepper flakes, garlic powder, and pepper. Place the pits back on top of the guacamole and cover with plastic directly on the surface to prevent browning.

When ready to serve, garnish with the nuts and the remaining half of the tomatoes.

Suggestions and Variations
Serve with red bell pepper planks, almond flour crackers, or low-carb chips.

Recipe Note
- Since tomatoes release water when in contact with salt, only stir in enough tomatoes for the amount of guacamole you will enjoy immediately to prevent a watered-down version. Or use drained, canned, diced tomatoes.
- When selecting perfectly ripe avocados, look for those with skins that are mottled with green and black. Then hold it in the palm of your hand and give it a gentle squeeze. A ripe avocado should yield to gentle pressure, but not be soft or mushy. If it's still completely hard, leave it on the counter for a couple more days.

TOTAL PREP AND COOK TIME: 20 MINUTES · YIELD: 8 SERVINGS, ¼ CUP (70 G) EACH

‹30

PER SERVING: 108 CALORIES, 7 G CARBOHYDRATE (4 G FIBER, 0 G ADDED SUGARS, 3 G NET CARBS), 2 G PROTEIN, 9 G FAT, 152 MG SODIUM.

SHRIMP-STUFFED MUSHROOMS WITH LEMON AND ROSEMARY

I find that baked stuffed mushrooms at parties always get devoured. And I love them, too. While the standard recipes are delicious, I wish they weren't mostly filled with cream cheese. In these stuffed mushrooms, I reverse the formula, using mostly shrimp and just a smidgen of good, real mayonnaise (or use cream cheese if you prefer).

1 pound (455 g) baby bella mushrooms (about 22 mushrooms)

1 tablespoon (15 ml) extra-virgin olive oil

½ teaspoon salt, divided

2 scallions, white and green parts, cut into 4 pieces, reserving 2 tablespoons (12 g) finely sliced green parts

1 clove garlic, peeled

¼ teaspoon dried rosemary

¾ pound (340 g) frozen peeled and deveined shrimp, thawed, tails removed

1 lemon, zest finely grated, then fruit cut into wedges, plus 1 teaspoon juice

2 tablespoons (28 g) mayonnaise

Freshly ground black pepper

Preheat the oven to 350°F (180°C, or gas mark 4). Line a large baking sheet with parchment paper.

Rinse the mushrooms briefly under running water, rubbing off any debris, and place on a towel. Pluck off the stems and slice off the bottom ⅛ inch (3 mm), just enough to remove any shriveled edges, reserving the plump parts of the stems. Place the mushroom caps on the baking sheet. Drizzle with the olive oil and sprinkle the insides with ¼ teaspoon of the salt.

Place the mushroom scraps, white and green scallion pieces (reserving the sliced scallions), garlic, and rosemary in a large food processor. Process until minced. Add the shrimp, lemon zest and juice, mayonnaise, remaining ¼ teaspoon salt, and pepper. Pulse about 10 times, until the shrimp is mostly finely chopped, with some small pieces remaining. Generously spoon the shrimp into the mushrooms, pressing lightly to fill the crevices. Smooth with the back of a spoon.

Bake until the mushrooms are tender and sizzling around the edges, about 15 minutes. Allow to rest a few minutes before serving. Sprinkle with the sliced scallions and serve with the lemon wedges.

Recipe Note
If you are feeding someone who doesn't eat mushrooms, you can form the shrimp mixture into patties and brown on both sides in a bit of oil over medium heat. Scrumptious.

TOTAL PREP AND COOK TIME: 45 MINUTES · YIELD: 22 SERVINGS, 1 MUSHROOM EACH

PER SERVING: 28 CALORIES, 1 G CARBOHYDRATE (0 G FIBER, 0 G ADDED SUGARS, 1 G NET CARBS), 3 G PROTEIN, 2 G FAT, 90 MG SODIUM.

LEBANESE MEAT PIES WITH GROUND BEEF AND LEMON

Growing up, a wonderfully bready, doughy version of these, called *fatayer*, could be found on the occasional snack tray in my *Sithoo*'s (grandmother's) kitchen. My version delivers an almond flour tart crust instead. Dollop the baked pies with sour cream or plain Greek yogurt for added deliciousness.

FOR THE DOUGH:

1 cup (123 g) almond flour, plus more for dusting

1 teaspoon baking powder

¼ teaspoon salt

2 tablespoons (30 ml) extra-virgin olive oil

3 large eggs

2 tablespoons (30 ml) milk

FOR THE FILLING:

1 pound (455 g) ground beef

½ medium onion, finely chopped

⅓ cup (80 ml) lemon juice

¼ teaspoon salt

Freshly ground black pepper

Preheat the oven to 350ºF (190ºC, or gas mark 4). Coat a muffin tin with cooking oil spray.

To make the dough: In a medium bowl, combine the flour, baking powder, and salt. Add the olive oil, eggs, and milk. Mix with a fork until a dough forms. On a large wood cutting board dusted with a bit of flour, roll out the dough to ⅛ inch (3 mm) thick, turning the dough occasionally with a turner or bench scraper to prevent sticking. Cut out twelve 4-inch (10 cm) circles. Gently press each circle into the muffin tin to fit into bottom edges. Bake for 15 minutes, until golden.

To make the filling: In a large bowl, combine all of the filling ingredients. Scoop ¼ cup meat into each crust, gently packing evenly. Bake 10–15 minutes, until the beef is cooked through.

TOTAL PREP AND COOK TIME: 45 MINUTES · YIELD: 12 SERVINGS, 1 EACH

PER SERVING: 190 CALORIES, 11 G CARBOHYDRATE (5 G FIBER, 0 G ADDED SUGARS, 6 G NET CARBS), 12 G PROTEIN, 11 G FAT, 195 MG SODIUM.

Clean Eating Kitchen: The Low-Carb Mediterranean Cookbook

3-INGREDIENT AVOCADO TRUFFLES WITH PISTACHIOS

You'll love the simplicity and ease of making these creamy, savory bites. Using avocados that are *just* ripe is key in this recipe, which means the fruit yields to gentle pressure, but is not soft. The skin should be speckly and blackish, with some green spots left.

3 tablespoons (27 g) shelled pistachios, finely chopped

1 teaspoon za'atar seasoning blend*

1 large just-ripe avocado

Combine the pistachios and za'atar in a wide, shallow container.

Using a ½-teaspoon measuring spoon that is half sphere–shaped, scoop the avocado to make an avocado ball, like you are scooping the perfect ball of ice cream. Fill any small gaps with avocado and smooth with a butter knife as needed. Roll the avocado ball gently in the pistachios to coat evenly. Repeat the process for the 11 other truffles. It is best to enjoy these on the same day that you make them.

Recipe Note

* Za'atar is a Middle Eastern spice blend that has been around for ages, yet has been trending recently. Made of mostly sesame seeds, thyme, sumac, and salt, it offers an aromatic and herbal taste. You can find it in well-stocked grocery stores or you can make your own. You can use up the rest of the bottle by sprinkling on roasted vegetables, chicken, and a plain yogurt dip drizzled with olive oil.

Suggestions and Variations

You can play around with the types of seasonings and nuts, like toasted walnuts or almonds.

TOTAL PREP AND COOK TIME: 20 MINUTES · YIELD: 12 SERVINGS, 1 BALL EACH

<30

PER SERVING: 30 CALORIES, 1 G CARBOHYDRATE (1 G FIBER, 0 G ADDED SUGARS, 0 G NET CARBS), 1 G PROTEIN, 3 G FAT, 4 MG SODIUM.

MINI BELL PEPPERS STUFFED WITH TURKEY AND PISTACHIOS

I *love* those raw sweet mini bell peppers for snacking. Just wash and eat! They also look adorable stuffed with ground turkey and roasted as little appetizers. You can prep these a day in advance and pop them into the oven right before party time.

1 bag (1-pound [455 g]) mini bell peppers (about 16)

¾ pound (340 g) ground turkey (93% lean)

⅓ cup (37 g) shelled pistachios, finely chopped, reserving 2 tablespoons (14 g)

2 teaspoons red wine vinegar

1 teaspoon ground cumin

½ teaspoon salt, divided

¼ teaspoon ground coriander (see Recipe Note)

¼ teaspoon ground cinnamon

Freshly ground black pepper

1 tablespoon (15 ml) extra-virgin olive oil

Preheat the oven to 400°F (200°C, or gas mark 6). Line a baking sheet with parchment paper.

Cut off the tops of the peppers right between the straight sides and the rounded shoulders. Pull out the seeds and membranes using your fingers or dislodge with a paring knife. Poke a hole into the pointy tips of the peppers, making an air gap to allow for easier stuffing.

In a medium bowl, combine the turkey, pistachios (reserving the 2 tablespoons [14 g]), vinegar, cumin, ¼ teaspoon salt, coriander, cinnamon, and pepper. Using a small spoon or butter knife, stuff the peppers with the turkey, leaving a nice rounded top protruding out a bit at the top of the peppers. Gently roll the meat ends of the peppers into the reserved pistachios. Place the peppers on the prepared baking sheet. Drizzle with the oil and sprinkle with the remaining ¼ teaspoon salt.

Bake until the largest peppers are blistered and tender, 15 to 20 minutes.

Recipe Note

My preferred way to buy coriander is as whole seeds and then grind only the amount I need with a mortar and pestle. It adds texture to the dish, where a fine powder can't. And the aroma is dreamy. It's one of my favorite spices, and I use it in Asian-style stir-fries, chilis, and meat rubs.

Suggestions and Variations

For a pepper-free version, you can shape the turkey into small patties and sauté in a bit of olive oil over medium heat.

TOTAL PREP AND COOK TIME: 30 MINUTES · YIELD: 16 SERVINGS, 1 PEPPER EACH

PER SERVING: 57 CALORIES, 2 G CARBOHYDRATE (1 G FIBER, 0 G ADDED SUGARS, 1 G NET CARBS), 5 G PROTEIN, 4 G FAT, 85 MG SODIUM.

MEDITERRANEAN QUINOA SALAD WITH AVOCADO

I adore quinoa salad, and you can prepare it in limitless varieties. Here is a Greek-themed play on it. Enjoy it as a side salad, or sprinkle cheese, beans, and nuts on top to make it a complete lunch meal.

¾ cup (139 g) uncooked quinoa

1⅓ cups (313 ml) vegetable broth

1 tablespoon (15 ml) extra-virgin olive oil

1 small cucumber, peeled, seeded, and diced

¼ teaspoon salt

Freshly ground black pepper

1 large tomato, diced

2 scallions, thinly sliced

2 tablespoons (8 g) coarsely chopped Italian flat-leaf parsley or mint

¼ cup (25 g) olives

1 large avocado, peeled, pitted, and diced

Juice of 1 lemon (about 2 tablespoons [30 ml])

Rinse the quinoa in a fine-mesh strainer, if you have one, and drain. Otherwise, skip this step. Bring the quinoa and broth to a boil in a saucepan. Reduce the heat to low, cover, and simmer for 15 minutes. Remove from the heat without lifting the lid and allow it to rest for 5 minutes. Drizzle with the olive oil, then spread it out on a plate to cool it quickly.

Add the cucumber, salt, pepper, tomato, scallions, parsley, and olives to a large mixing bowl. Add the quinoa once it has cooled to room temperature. Gently fold in the avocado and lemon juice.

Suggestions and Variations

• Sprinkle in pomegranate arils during peak season, which runs mid-late fall through early winter, in place of the tomatoes. The arils add a juicy, poppy crunch.
• If you love feta cheese, a sprinkle of that in this salad is also delicious.
• Roasted pistachios or almonds sprinkled on this salad add a nice crunch.

TOTAL PREP AND COOK TIME: 30 MINUTES · YIELD: 8 SERVINGS, ½ CUP (125 G) EACH

PER SERVING: 125 CALORIES, 16 G CARBOHYDRATE (3 G FIBER, 0 G ADDED SUGARS, 13 G NET CARBS), 3 G PROTEIN, 6 G FAT, 205 MG SODIUM.

CAESAR SALAD WITH TAHINI-GARLIC DRESSING AND PARMESAN CRISPS

One of the most favorite salads on the planet is Caesar. I love everything about it: the creamy, Parmy dressing. The crunchy, salty croutons. And crisp romaine. So why not add one more take to the dish, with a tahini-based salad dressing instead of egg, and Parmesan crisps in place of croutons.

FOR THE DRESSING:

2 tablespoons (31 g) tahini

1 tablespoon (15 ml) lemon juice

3 tablespoons (45 ml) water

2 teaspoons Dijon mustard

⅛ teaspoon salt

Freshly ground black pepper

Minced anchovies (optional)

FOR THE SALAD:

1 clove garlic, halved

1 head romaine lettuce, ribs removed, torn

⅓ cup (13 g) Parmesan crisps, store-bought or homemade (page 60)

3 tablespoons (8 g) grated Parmesan cheese

Salt and freshly ground black pepper

½ cup (75 g) cherry tomatoes, halved

To make the dressing: In a small bowl, whisk together all of the dressing ingredients.

To make the salad: Rub the mixing bowl with the cut sides of the garlic. Place the romaine and Parmesan crisps in the bowl and drizzle on the dressing. Sprinkle with Parmesan, salt, and pepper, to taste. Toss, coating evenly. Plate the salad and garnish with the tomatoes.

Recipe Note

If you love anchovies like my husband and I do, you can mince them and stir into the dressing and garnish with some on the side. Plus, they are so good for you!

TOTAL PREP AND COOK TIME: 30 MINUTES IF MAKING PARMESAN CRISPS · YIELD: 2 SERVINGS

<30 PER SERVING: 227 CALORIES, 13 G CARBOHYDRATE (4 G FIBER, 0 G ADDED SUGARS, 9 G NET CARBS), 12 G PROTEIN, 16 G FAT, 693 MG SODIUM.

BAKED KIBBEH WITH QUINOA, MINT, AND LEMON

Traditionally, *kibbeh* is mixed with fine wheat bulgur, but for this recipe I use quinoa, since it's gluten-free and you're likely to already have it on hand.

¼ cup (60 ml) extra-virgin olive oil, divided, plus more for drizzling

½ cup (67 g) pine nuts or slivered almonds (55 g)

1 pound (455 g) ground chuck or lean ground beef, divided

½ medium onion, half finely chopped and half cut into chunks

1 lemon, zest finely grated, then fruit cut into wedges

½ teaspoon salt, divided

Freshly ground black pepper

½ cup (86 g) uncooked quinoa

½ cup (120 ml) beef or chicken broth

1 teaspoon dried mint, plus more for garnish

Fresh Italian flat-leaf parsley or mint, coarsely chopped or torn

Flaky sea salt

Preheat the oven to 350°F (180°C, or gas mark 4). Drizzle the bottom and sides of a 9 × 9-inch (23 × 23-cm) baking dish with 1 tablespoon (15 ml) of the oil.

Heat a sauté pan over medium heat. Add the nuts and toast until they begin to turn golden, about 3 minutes. Add 1 tablespoon (15 ml) of the oil, one-fourth of the beef, and the chopped onion. Brown for about 5 minutes. Stir in the lemon zest, ¼ teaspoon of the salt, and pepper. Remove from the heat.

Blend the quinoa in a blender until it is cracked into smaller pieces, about 5 to 10 seconds. Cover completely with warm water. Drain and add more water. Grab small fistfuls of wet quinoa and squeeze the water out, placing back into the bowl.

Puree the onion chunks and broth in the blender. Add to a large mixing bowl. Add the remaining three-fourths of the beef, remaining ¼ teaspoon salt, pepper, and mint to the bowl. Mix well with your hands or a fork.

Spread nearly half of the raw beef in the pan; a fork works well to spread it out. Top with the cooked beef. Then top with the remaining raw beef and smooth out.

TOTAL PREP AND COOK TIME: 60 MINUTES · YIELD: 16 SERVINGS, 1 PIECE EACH

PER SERVING: 139 CALORIES, 5 G CARBOHYDRATE (1 G FIBER, 0 G ADDED SUGARS, 4 G NET CARBS), 7 G PROTEIN, 11 G FAT, 115 MG SODIUM

Cut the beef completely through into 1-inch (2.5 cm) strips in one direction. Then cut diagonally to make diamond shapes. Stick the knife through each piece so the layers don't separate. Cut around all sides of the pan. Drizzle with the remaining 2 tablespoons (30 ml) oil.

Bake until the beef is cooked through in the middle, about 30 minutes. Allow to cool for 5 minutes before cutting into pieces.

Garnish with coarsely chopped parsley or mint and flaky sea salt. Drizzle with oil.

TABBOULEH SALAD WITH CHICKPEAS AND QUINOA

Tabbouleh salad was always present at my grandma's house while I was growing up, but it was different from what I see in stores today. Traditional tabbouleh is more of a green parsley salad with just small flecks of wheat bulgur, rather than the opposite ratio you find in grocery stores.

Since I rarely seem to have luck finding fine wheat bulgur in stores, I went straight to quinoa in this recipe.

¼ cup (43 g) uncooked quinoa (makes 1 cup cooked and fluffed)

½ cup (120 ml) vegetable broth

1 (15-ounce [425 g]) can chickpeas, rinsed and drained

2 bunches Italian flat-leaf parsley, leaves picked from stems (about 4 cups [240 g] lightly packed)

2 Roma tomatoes, chopped small

¼ cup (40 g) finely diced onion

Juice of 1 lemon (about 2 tablespoons [30 ml])

2 tablespoons (30 ml) extra-virgin olive oil

¼ teaspoon salt

Freshly ground black pepper

Rinse the quinoa in a fine-mesh strainer, if you have one, and drain. Otherwise, skip this step. Bring the quinoa and broth to a boil in a saucepan. Reduce the heat to low and cover. Cook until tender, about 15 minutes. Remove from the heat and allow to sit for 5 minutes undisturbed. Spread out on a plate, running lines through it with a spoon to cool quickly.

In a bowl, combine the cooled quinoa, chickpeas, parsley, tomatoes, onion, lemon juice, oil, salt, and pepper. Serve chilled or at room temperature.

Suggestions and Variations
If you're eating a big bowl of this like I do for a meal, try sprinkling on crumbled feta cheese for added flavor, protein, and calcium.

TOTAL PREP AND COOK TIME: 30 MINUTES · YIELD: 8 SERVINGS, ½ CUP (100 G) EACH

PER SERVING: 105 CALORIES, 12 G CARBOHYDRATE (3 G FIBER, 0 G ADDED SUGARS, 9 G NET CARBS), 4 G PROTEIN, 5 G FAT, 150 MG SODIUM.

SHIRAZI SALAD

This Iranian salad, used like a condiment, is a staple in my sister Lauren's kitchen, since it complements meat dishes nicely, with crisp, cool vegetables and a big hit of lemon. Or you can use limes instead.

   Toss this salad right before mealtime if you prefer things extra crunchy, which is how my Iranian neighbor Sarah prefers it. Or mix it a few hours in advance if you like a more marinated salad.

½ large English cucumber or 2 small
   Persian cucumbers, diced small

1 medium tomato or 2 Roma tomatoes,
   diced small

2 tablespoons (2 g) cilantro leaves,
   coarsely chopped

1 teaspoon dried mint

⅛ medium red onion, thinly sliced

1 tablespoon (15 ml) extra-virgin
   olive oil

2 tablespoons (60 ml) lemon juice

1 small serrano chile pepper, seeded
   and thinly sliced (this is a hot
   pepper, adjust as needed)

¼ teaspoon salt

Freshly ground black pepper

Combine all of the ingredients in a mixing bowl.
Enjoy right away or cover and chill until ready to serve.

Suggestions and Variations
Jalapeño chile pepper or bell pepper may be a more suitable option if you prefer foods with less heat.

TOTAL PREP AND COOK TIME: 15 MINUTES · YIELD: 6 SERVINGS, ½ CUP (100 G) EACH

PER SERVING: 63 CALORIES, 5 G CARBOHYDRATE (1 G FIBER, 0 G ADDED SUGARS, 4 G NET CARBS), 1 G PROTEIN, 5 G FAT, 102 MG SODIUM.

BREAKFAST SALAD

For New Year's, my husband resolved to eat a salad for lunch every day. Currently we are in May, and he is still holding strong, which I think is pretty amazing. On the days he has his heart set on a sandwich instead, he eats this breakfast salad that he created. I have to say, it is really delicious and satisfying.

The key to this is cooking the eggs just until the whites are done, but with the yolks still runny, since that becomes the dressing. In our house, when cooking for just myself, I use my trusty microwave egg poacher, which cooks eggs close to perfectly in under 1 minute.

1 large egg (or 2 if you are extra hungry)

2 cups (60 g) baby arugula or spinach

⅓ large avocado, peeled, pitted, and diced

Juice of 1 lemon wedge

Pinch of salt

Freshly ground black pepper

Cook the eggs with your preferred method—either sunny-side up or poached—with the yolks still runny.

Place the arugula, avocado, lemon juice, salt, and pepper in a mixing bowl. Add the eggs, breaking them up so the yolk releases. Toss.

Suggestions and Variations

You can certainly embellish this salad with other ingredients you have on hand, like cherry tomatoes and leftover bits of protein from dinner, such as beans or chopped pieces of meat.

TOTAL PREP AND COOK TIME: 10 MINUTES · YIELD: 1 SERVING

<30

PER SERVING: 150 CALORIES, 7 G CARBOHYDRATE (4 G FIBER, 0 G ADDED SUGARS, 3 G NET CARBS), 8 G PROTEIN, 11 G FAT, 232 MG SODIUM.

SIMPLE GREEN SALAD WITH TOMATOES, CUCUMBERS, AND LEMON-MINT VINAIGRETTE

This salad was a staple served at most large family gatherings at my grandma Helen's while I was growing up. The light acidity of this salad balances perfectly with meats, dips, and seafood. My cousin Jenn has kept our Lebanese family's tradition going by preparing it every time I visit. My grandma always used iceberg lettuce, but my cousin and I *zhuzh* it up with other greens. Toss only the amount of salad you'll need in one sitting with the vinaigrette, to maintain crispness.

FOR THE VINAIGRETTE:

Juice of 1 lemon (about 2 tablespoons [30 ml])

2 tablespoons (30 ml) extra-virgin olive oil

½ teaspoon dried mint

⅛ teaspoon salt

FOR THE SALAD:

4 to 5 cups (220 to 275 g) torn or chopped Bibb or romaine lettuce (or use an Italian blend mix)

1 medium tomato, diced or sliced and quartered

½ medium cucumber, peeled, halved lengthwise, and sliced (about ¾ cup [89 g])

Salt and freshly ground black pepper

To make the vinaigrette: In a jar with a tight-fitting lid, combine all of the vinaigrette ingredients and shake.

To make the salad: In a bowl, combine the lettuce, tomato, and cumber. Drizzle the dressing over the greens. Season with an additional pinch of salt, to taste, and pepper. Toss evenly and gently.

Recipe Note

The vinaigrette makes enough for about two extra servings of salad. Therefore, you can either bulk up the salad recipe a bit or reserve the vinaigrette for other dishes, like seafood.

TOTAL PREP AND COOK TIME: 20 MINUTES · YIELD: 4 SERVINGS, 1 CUP (60 G) EACH (WITH 1 TEASPOON VINAIGRETTE)

PER SERVING: 80 CALORIES, 4 G CARBOHYDRATE (2 G FIBER, 0 G ADDED SUGARS, 2 G NET CARBS), 1 G PROTEIN, 7 G FAT, 80 MG SODIUM.

CUCUMBER YOGURT SALAD

In my *Sithoo*'s house, *leben* was as much a staple as ketchup was in other homes. She made it by simmering whole milk until it was "so hot that you couldn't hold your pinky finger in it," as she liked to explain, followed by squeezing the liquid from the curd while wrapped in cheesecloth.

I think you will appreciate the shortcut I use in this recipe—head straight for the store-bought Greek yogurt! To make it extra rich and delicious, I use 2% or whole-milk yogurt, rather than nonfat yogurt.

1 medium cucumber, peeled and sliced into half-moons (1 ¾ cups [210 g])

½ cup (115 g) 2% plain Greek yogurt, pouring off any liquid from the top

1 scallion, thinly sliced

2 teaspoons white wine vinegar

½ teaspoon salt

Combine all of the ingredients in a bowl. You may enjoy the salad immediately or chill until ready to serve, pouring off any liquid.

Recipe Note

A hard-core purist would salt the cucumbers first, let them sit for 30 minutes, then pat off the liquid released. That's just not my style. I'm hungry and pretty much want things ready instantly. After pulling the salad from the fridge, however, I *will* drain off the excess liquid. If you'd like to go the purist route, however, just wait to add more salt to the salad until you've tasted it first.

TOTAL PREP AND COOK TIME: 15 MINUTES · YIELD: 5 SERVINGS, ¼ CUP (60 G) EACH

PER SERVING: 24 CALORIES, 2 G CARBOHYDRATE (0 G FIBER, 0 G ADDED SUGARS, 2 G NET CARBS), 3 G PROTEIN, 1 G FAT, 242 MG SODIUM.

TOMATO AND CUCUMBER CHOPPED SALAD

I love the freshness and crunch of this bright-tasting salad.

1 medium cucumber, diced (1½ cups [205 g])

1 medium tomato, diced (1 cup [180 g])

1 scallion, thinly sliced

1 tablespoon (15 ml) extra-virgin olive oil

1 tablespoon (15 ml) red wine vinegar

½ teaspoon dried mint

½ teaspoon dried dill

⅛ teaspoon garlic powder

⅛ teaspoon salt

Freshly ground black pepper

¼ cup (37 g) crumbled feta cheese

Gently combine all of the ingredients in a mixing bowl, except the feta. Fold in the feta.

Suggestions and Variations
If you have fresh mint or dill on hand, by all means, use it. Fresh Italian flat-leaf parsley or basil would also pair nicely.

TOTAL PREP AND COOK TIME: 15 MINUTES · YIELD: 4 SERVINGS, ½ CUP (100 G) EACH

PER SERVING: 72 CALORIES, 4 G CARBOHYDRATE (1 G FIBER, 0 G ADDED SUGARS, 3 G NET CARBS), 2 G PROTEIN, 6 G FAT, 184 MG SODIUM.

TUNA AVOCADO SALAD

I love the simplicity of cracking open a can of tuna, adding a few seasonings, and calling it lunch, especially in the summer. For a richer taste, buy canned tuna in olive oil.

You can create all sorts of different lunch plates with this protein-rich centerpiece. Pair with arugula, tomatoes, a sprinkle of chickpeas, toasted nuts, chopped herbs like parsley or basil, olives, or capers. Or all of the above if you're extra hungry!

1 (5-ounce [567 g]) can tuna, drained well

⅓ large ripe avocado, peeled, pitted, and diced

1 tablespoon (15 ml) extra-virgin olive oil

1½ teaspoons balsamic vinegar

⅛ teaspoon garlic powder

⅛ teaspoon onion powder

⅛ teaspoon salt

Freshly ground black pepper

Break up the tuna in a bowl with a fork. Add the remaining ingredients and stir.

TOTAL PREP AND COOK TIME: 10 MINUTES · YIELD: 1 SERVING

PER SERVING: 306 CALORIES, 5 G CARBOHYDRATE (3 G FIBER, 0 G ADDED SUGARS, 2 G NET CARBS), 25 G PROTEIN, 21 G FAT, 600 MG SODIUM.

LENTIL FATTOUSH SALAD WITH CARAMELIZED RED ONIONS

Fattoush salad—one of my favorites—is a Middle Eastern salad traditionally made of lettuce, tomatoes, cucumbers, and pita. In this recipe, I eliminate the pita and add flavor with sun-dried tomatoes and by cooking lentils in vegetable broth, adding layers of *umami*. Only mix the amount of salad you'll eat in one sitting to maintain the texture. For added crunch, sprinkle on baked cheese crisps.

FOR THE ONIONS:

2 teaspoons extra-virgin olive oil

½ medium red onion, thinly sliced into rings

FOR THE LENTILS:

½ cup (96 g) dried green or brown lentils

1 cup (235 ml) vegetable broth

FOR THE VINAIGRETTE:

1 lemon, ½ zested, all of it juiced

½ teaspoon Dijon mustard

1 clove garlic, peeled, halved

¼ teaspoon ground cumin

Pinch of salt

¼ cup (60 ml) extra-virgin olive oil

FOR THE SALAD:

1 head romaine lettuce, leaves torn from ribs

8 sun-dried tomato halves in oil, chopped

Salt and freshly ground black pepper

To make the onions: Heat a medium sauté pan over medium heat. Add the oil and when it begins to shimmer, add the onions. Stir and reduce the heat to low. Slowly cook, stirring occasionally, while you prep the rest of the ingredients. Remove from the heat when the onions are very tender and soft, about 15 minutes.

To make the lentils: In a medium pot, cover the lentils with water, pulling out any foreign objects, and drain. Pour in the vegetable broth over the lentils and bring to a boil over medium-high heat. Reduce the heat to low, cover, and simmer until tender, about 15 minutes. Drain off excess liquid.

To make the vinaigrette: Place the lemon juice, zest, Dijon, garlic halves, cumin, and salt in a jar with tight-sealing lid. Shake until blended well. Add the oil and shake again.

To make the salad: Place the romaine, onions, sun-dried tomatoes, a pinch of salt, and pepper in a mixing bowl. Only dress the amount of salad you plan on eating in one sitting and refrigerate the rest. Drizzle with the proportionate amount of vinaigrette, about 1½ tablespoons (23 ml) per serving. Toss to coat evenly. Arrange the salad in bowls and spoon the lentils on top, drizzling with a bit more vinaigrette.

TOTAL PREP AND COOK TIME: 40 MINUTES · YIELD: 4 SERVINGS

PER SERVING: 257 CALORIES, 22 G CARBOHYDRATE (8 G FIBER, 0 G ADDED SUGARS, 14 G NET CARBS), 8 G PROTEIN, 18 G FAT, 397 MG SODIUM.

SALMON SALAD WITH DILL, CAPERS, AND ARTICHOKE

If you enjoy canned salmon like I do, you will love having this lunchtime salad over greens, with vegetable crudités, or in a lettuce wrap.

1 (14.75-ounce [418 g]) can salmon, drained well

1 (14-ounce [396 g]) can quartered artichoke hearts, drained

¼ cup (60 ml) extra-virgin olive oil

3 tablespoons (45 ml) red wine vinegar

1 tablespoon (7.5 g) capers

½ teaspoon dried dill

¼ teaspoon salt

Freshly ground black pepper

In a mixing bowl, break up the salmon into smaller bits with a fork. Trim any tough outer tips from the artichokes, then cut the hearts into bite-size pieces. Combine all of the ingredients in the bowl. You may enjoy right away or cover and chill until ready to serve. This salad keeps nicely for up to 5 days in the refrigerator.

Recipe Note
- I prefer to peel away the skin of the salmon first. However, I do leave in the bones, which are edible and crumbly in canned salmon, and contribute a significant amount of calcium, too.
- The outer tips of the artichoke leaves can be a bit tough and fibrous, even in canned artichokes, so I trim those off.

TOTAL PREP AND COOK TIME: 20 MINUTES · YIELD: 4 SERVINGS, ABOUT ¾ CUP (175 G) EACH

PER SERVING: 292 CALORIES, 5 G CARBOHYDRATE (3 G FIBER, 0 G ADDED SUGARS, 2 G NET CARBS), 26 G PROTEIN, 19 G FAT, 710 MG SODIUM.

CARAMELIZED ONION AND RED LENTIL SOUP

I whipped up this soup one wintry day using just simple ingredients I already had on hand. Such warming results! Healthy comfort food and totally vegan.

Rest assured, while some dried legumes take a while to cook, lentils only take 15 minutes to simmer; then they are tender and ready to eat.

2 tablespoons (30 ml) extra-virgin olive oil, plus more for drizzling

1 medium carrot, thinly sliced

1 cup (160 g) diced onion

1 clove garlic, thinly sliced

½ teaspoon ground cumin

½ teaspoon sweet paprika

¼ teaspoon dried oregano

1 cup (192 g) dried red lentils, rinsed a few times, drained

4 cups (950 ml) vegetable broth

4 lemon slices

Salt and freshly ground black pepper

Place a soup pot over medium heat. Add the oil. When the oil is shimmering, add the carrot, onion, and garlic, reduce the heat to medium-low, and cook until tender, about 5 minutes. Add the cumin, paprika, and oregano and cook until aromatic, about 30 seconds. Add the lentils and broth. Cover with a lid slightly ajar, and simmer until the lentils are tender, about 15 minutes. Turn off the heat and add the lemon slices. Taste the soup to see if you'd like to add salt and pepper or not, as the saltiness of vegetable broth varies.

Ladle the soup into bowls and drizzle with more oil for added richness.

Nutrition Note

- While a serving of lentils (¼ cup [48 g] dried) contains 32 grams total carbohydrate, it delivers a whopping 14 grams fiber and 13 grams protein, giving you only 18 grams net carbs. And with 20 percent of the Daily Value for iron, lentils are very nourishing.
- At just about 30 cents per serving of red lentils, who says that eating healthy has to be expensive?

TOTAL PREP AND COOK TIME: 30 MINUTES · YIELD: 4 SERVINGS, 1 CUP (250 G) EACH

PER SERVING: 287 CALORIES, 40 G CARBOHYDRATE (15 G FIBER, 0 G ADDED SUGARS, 25 G NET CARBS), 14 G PROTEIN, 7 G FAT, 576 MG SODIUM.

KALE SALAD WITH BLUEBERRIES AND FETA

Kale and blueberries may seem like an unlikely pairing, but trust me, it works! The key to tender kale is to massage the vinaigrette into the greens and allow it to sit before enjoying. You can mix the entire batch and enjoy for the next couple of days, reserving the walnuts until ready to eat, to preserve crunchiness.

½ cup (60 g) walnuts, chopped

1 (5-ounce [142 g]) bag kale

1 tablespoon (15 ml) red wine vinegar (or use fresh orange juice if you prefer things sweeter)

¼ teaspoon salt

2 tablespoons (30 ml) extra-virgin olive oil

1 tablespoon (14 g) mayonnaise

Freshly ground black pepper

½ cup (75 g) crumbled feta cheese

½ pint blueberries (about 1 cup [145 g])

Toast the walnuts in a sauté pan over medium heat until aromatic and golden, stirring frequently, about 7 minutes.

Place the kale in a medium-size bowl. Drizzle with the vinegar and sprinkle with the salt. Massage the vinegar into the kale with your hands for about 1 minute. Add the oil, mayonnaise, and pepper, and toss with tongs. Sprinkle in the feta and walnuts and toss. Sprinkle in the blueberries and toss gently with a spoon.

TOTAL PREP AND COOK TIME: 20 MINUTES · YIELD: 4 SERVINGS, 1 CUP (80 G) EACH

<30 PER SERVING: 248 CALORIES, 9 G CARBOHYDRATE (3 G FIBER, 0 G ADDED SUGARS, 6 G NET CARBS), 6 G PROTEIN, 22 G FAT, 400 MG SODIUM.

SHRIMP SALAD WITH AVOCADOS AND TOMATOES

My husband came up with this recipe, inspired by the number of fresh and simple salads we've enjoyed in the Mediterranean. He whips it up effortlessly for lunch on the weekends, of which I am always very appreciative. He is my weekend "chef"! He normally sautés raw shrimp, but here I saved you a step by buying precooked shrimp.

Also, Delicia, a top Spanish restaurant in Indianapolis, Indiana, makes a version of this salad with lump crab and ground aji chili, so I encourage you to get creative with which kind of shellfish and chili powder you use.

½ pound (225 g) cooked medium shrimp, tails removed, each cut Into 3 pieces

1 scallion, thinly sliced

1 tablespoon (15 ml) lemon juice

1 tablespoon (14 g) mayonnaise

¼ teaspoon chili powder

⅛ teaspoon salt, plus an additional pinch for the greens

Freshly ground black pepper

⅔ large ripe avocado, peeled, pitted, and diced

4 cups (80 g) baby arugula or other mixed greens

Vinaigrette (store-bought) for the greens, or drizzle lightly with red wine vinegar and extra-virgin olive oil

½ cup (75 g) cherry tomatoes, halved

¼ cup (28 g) shelled pistachios, chopped through once or twice

In a mixing bowl, combine the shrimp, scallion, lemon juice, mayonnaise, chili powder, salt, and pepper. Add the avocado and stir a few times to incorporate, while leaving it chunky.

Place the greens in a separate mixing bowl. Dress lightly with your favorite vinaigrette or vinegar and oil, plus a pinch of salt and pepper. Toss.

To plate, place the greens in wide, shallow bowls. Scoop the shrimp salad, placing it in the middle, and arrange the tomatoes all around. Sprinkle with the pistachios.

TOTAL PREP AND COOK TIME: 30 MINUTES · YIELD: 2 SERVINGS

<30

PER SERVING: 293 CALORIES, 11 G CARBOHYDRATE (6 G FIBER, 0 G ADDED SUGARS, 5 G NET CARBS), 21 G PROTEIN, 20 G FAT, 765 MG SODIUM.

ARUGULA SALAD WITH CALAMARI, ZUCCHINI, AND BALSAMIC

The inspiration for this recipe stems from the restaurant Barba Danilo, in lovely Rovinj, Croatia, a town on the Adriatic Sea that my husband and I visited.

FOR THE BALSAMIC:

¼ cup (60 ml) balsamic vinegar

1 teaspoon honey

FOR THE CALAMARI:

1 pound (455 g) calamari, thawed, patted dry

2 teaspoons extra-virgin olive oil

1 clove garlic, smashed once with wide side of knife, skin removed

¼ teaspoon salt

Pinch of red pepper flakes

2 teaspoons lemon juice

FOR THE SALAD:

1 small zucchini, thinly sliced

1 tablespoon (15 ml) extra-virgin olive oil

⅛ teaspoon salt

8 cups (160 g) baby arugula

2 ounces (55 g) Manchego, Parmesan, or Asiago cheese, thinly sliced (about 12 slices)

8 sun-dried tomatoes in oil, sliced

Freshly ground black pepper

To make the balsamic: Pour the balsamic into a small saucepan and bring to a simmer over medium heat. Simmer until the balsamic reduces by about half, about 4 minutes. Remove from the heat and stir in the honey.

To make the calamari: Slice the calamari bodies into ¼-inch (6 mm) thick rings, and cut large tentacles down the middle to ensure even cooking. Heat a large sauté pan over medium-high heat. Add the oil to the pan and when the oil starts shimmering, add the calamari, garlic, salt and pepper flakes. Sauté until the calamari is opaque white and cooked through, about 4 minutes. Transfer the calamari to a plate using a slotted spoon. Put the pan with the juices back on the heat to evaporate until it's thickened so that when you draw a spoon through it, the line remains, about 3 minutes of cooking. Drizzle the juices over the calamari and spritz with lemon juice.

To make the salad: Spread the zucchini out on a plate. Drizzle with the olive oil and season with salt. Arrange half of the zucchini slices on a platter or in shallow bowls. Place the arugula on top and drizzle with the balsamic. Arrange the remaining zucchini over the arugula, followed by the cheese on top. Place the tomatoes around the edges of the salad. Spoon the calamari on the very top of the salad. Season with pepper.

TOTAL PREP AND COOK TIME: 30 MINUTES · YIELD: 4 SERVINGS

PER SERVING: 284 CALORIES, 11 G CARBOHYDRATE (3 G FIBER, 1 G ADDED SUGARS, 8 G NET CARBS), 25 G PROTEIN, 18 G FAT, 703 MG SODIUM.

WHITE BEAN AND VEGETABLE MINESTRONE

I adore cozying up to a piping hot bowl of homemade soup. Does it get any better than that on a chilly day? When you're already hungry, though, making soup from scratch may seem time-consuming, but not with this recipe! It's ready in less than 30 minutes. It's light, packed with vegetables, and has some white beans for added staying power.

2 tablespoons (30 ml) extra-virgin olive oil, plus more for drizzling

1 medium carrot, diced (½ cup [65 g])

1 stalk celery, diced (½ cup [50 g])

½ medium red onion, diced (about 1 cup [160 g])

1 clove garlic, smashed with wide side of knife, skin removed

½ teaspoon salt, divided

Freshly ground black pepper

4 cups (268 g) chopped kale

3 cups (705 ml) vegetable broth

1 can (14.5 ounces, [411 g]) diced tomatoes

1 teaspoon Italian seasoning

1 teaspoon apple cider vinegar

1 can (15.8-ounce [448 g]) white beans (like Great Northern or cannellini), rinsed and drained

Place a soup pot over medium heat. Add the oil. When the oil is shimmering, add the carrot, celery, onion, garlic, ¼ teaspoon of the salt, and pepper and cook until tender, about 10 minutes. Halfway through cooking the vegetables, add the kale.

Add the broth and tomatoes with juice, Italian seasoning, remaining ¼ teaspoon salt, and pepper. Simmer for 10 more minutes to blend the flavors. Stir in the apple cider vinegar. Ladle into bowls and drizzle with more olive oil.

<30

TOTAL PREP AND COOK TIME: 30 MINUTES · YIELD: 5 SERVINGS, 1 CUP (235 G) EACH

PER SERVING: 182 CALORIES, 26 G CARBOHYDRATE (8 G FIBER, 0 G ADDED SUGARS, 18 G NET CARBS), 7 G PROTEIN, 7 G FAT, 892 MG SODIUM.

EASY GAZPACHO

A good gazpacho is so refreshing. While the ingredients and technique are simple, good-quality olive oil and ripe tomatoes give it a richer taste. I tend to buy the vine-on tomatoes when I'm buying tomatoes from the grocery store. If the tomatoes aren't fully ripe, put them on a sunny windowsill for a day or two before using.

4 smallish medium-ripe tomatoes, cored

½ English cucumber, peeled

1 red bell pepper, cut into chunks

½ cup (55 g) slivered or skinless sliced almonds

¼ red onion

¼ cup (10 g) basil leaves

1 clove garlic, peeled

2 teaspoons sherry vinegar

½ teaspoon salt

Freshly ground black pepper

¼ cup (60 ml) extra-virgin olive oil

Bring a pot of water to a boil. Fill a bowl with ice water. Score the tomatoes with a paring knife, making an X on the end opposite the core. Using tongs, carefully place the tomatoes in the water to blanch them. When the peel starts pulling away, about 30 seconds, transfer the tomatoes to the ice water. Peel off the skins. Quarter the tomatoes.

Place all of the ingredients in a blender, except the oil, up to three-fourths of the way full. Do not overfill. Add enough water to fill to about halfway to where the vegetables are, just enough to get the vegetables moving in the blender. You may need to blend in batches, combining in a big bowl. Puree on low speed, working your way up to high. It should be smoothie consistency, so add more water, if needed. Drizzle in the oil while blending on low speed. Chill until ready to serve.

Suggestions and Variations

Serving this in shallow, wide bowls looks pretty if you are garnishing with bits like diced avocado or poached shrimp.

TOTAL PREP AND COOK TIME: 30 MINUTES · YIELD: 6 SERVINGS, 1 CUP (235 ML) EACH

PER SERVING: 160 CALORIES, 9 G CARBOHYDRATE (3 G FIBER, 0 G ADDED SUGARS, 6 G NET CARBS), 3 G PROTEIN, 14 G FAT, 200 MG SODIUM.

CRISPY ROASTED CHICKPEAS

These are the perfect antidote to a crunchy, salty, snack craving, plus you're getting protein, fiber, iron, and the goodness of beans. These crisp chickpeas can also be enjoyed over salads, soups, and cottage cheese, adding texture.

1 can (15-ounce [425 g]) chickpeas, drained and rinsed well

2 tablespoons (30 ml) extra-virgin olive oil

¼ teaspoon kosher salt

Freshly ground black pepper

1 teaspoon ground sumac

Preheat the oven to 350°F (180°C, or gas mark 4) convection. Line a baking sheet with parchment paper.

After rinsing and draining the chickpeas, pour them onto a clean towel and move the towel back and forth on the countertop to dry the chickpeas. This thorough drying helps crisp the chickpeas during baking.

Place the chickpeas on the prepared baking sheet and drizzle with the olive oil. Sprinkle with the salt and pepper. Roast until golden and crispy, about 40 minutes. Sprinkle with the sumac. Allow them to cool completely before sealing them in a container. The longer they can sit uncovered and dry out, the better.

Suggestions and Variations

Feel free to play around with different spices on these, like turmeric, curry powder, cumin, and chili powder.

TOTAL PREP AND COOK TIME: 40 MINUTES · YIELD: 4 SERVINGS, ¼ CUP (100 G) EACH

PER SERVING: 120 CALORIES, 9 G CARBOHYDRATE (3 G FIBER, 0 G ADDED SUGARS, 6 G NET CARBS), 3 G PROTEIN, 8 G FAT, 189 MG SODIUM.

"EVERYTHING" BAKED PARMESAN CRISPS

These crispy, crunchy *umami* bombs are so easy to make. Enjoy them as a snack or sprinkle over salads and soups.

1 cup (100 g) grated Parmesan cheese

1 tablespoon (12 g) "everything" seasoning

Preheat the oven to 350°F (180°C, or gas mark 4). Line a large baking sheet with a silicone baking mat.

Place piles of 1 tablespoon (6 g) cheese on the prepared baking sheet, spreading each out to at least 1 inch (2.5 cm) wide in a solid circle (you can use a cookie cutter if that makes your life easier). Sprinkle with the seasoning. Bake until the cheese becomes deep golden, 12 to 15 minutes. They will crisp as they cool.

Suggestions and Variations

Try other seasonings, too, like smoked paprika, garlic powder, and onion powder.

TOTAL PREP AND COOK TIME: 30 MINUTES · YIELD: 4 SERVINGS, 4 CRISPS EACH

PER SERVING: 84 CALORIES, 3 G CARBOHYDRATE (0 G FIBER, 0 G ADDED SUGARS, 3 G NET CARBS), 6 G PROTEIN, 6 G FAT, 570 MG SODIUM.

ROSÉ SPRITZ WITH CITRUS AND MINT

One sip of this light rosé spritz and you might feel like you should be on the Mediterranean. While vacationing in Rovinj, Croatia (a little seaside village in the northern part of the country, in Istria—the truffle mecca), I enjoyed a wine cocktail very similar to this one. I made a few modifications to eliminate any need for simple syrups, an ingredient usually used to sweeten drinks.

1 large mint sprig, leaves removed from stems

2 orange slices

Crushed ice

5 ounces (150 ml) rosé wine

2 teaspoons elderflower liqueur (optional)

2 ounces (60 ml) grapefruit-flavored sparkling water

Place the mint leaves and orange slices in a glass (I prefer to use a sturdy stemless wineglass). Smash them gently a few times with a muddler or wooden spoon, pressing out the juices. Add the crushed ice and rosé. Top with the liqueur, if using, and sparkling water.

Suggestions and Variations
This drink is also delicious made with dry white wine, such as Sauvignon Blanc, in place of rosé.

Make It for the Whole Family
For the kiddies, make mocktails with 100 percent fruit juice in place of the wine and liqueur.

TOTAL PREP AND COOK TIME: 10 MINUTES · YIELD: 1 SERVING

PER SERVING: 140 CALORIES, 3 G CARBOHYDRATE (1 G FIBER, 0 G ADDED SUGARS, 2 G NET CARBS), 0 G PROTEIN, 0 G FAT, 14 MG SODIUM.

FRESH MINT TEA WITH CITRUS

This hot drink is a digestif, rather than an aperitif, and is a soothing, comforting way to end the day after a meal. It's a great way to use up an abundance of fresh mint. I love using my double-walled glass teacup for this, which seems to stay hotter, longer.

1 cup (240 ml) water

1 small handful fresh mint leaves

1 lime slice

1 orange slice

Bring the water to a boil in a kettle. Place the mint in the teacup. Pour the boiling water over the mint. Add the lime and orange slices. Cover with a saucer and allow it to steep. After a few minutes, you can start drinking it while it's hottest. Press gently on the orange and lime to release some of the juices.

You can remove the mint and citrus before sipping or leave them in the glass to steep longer to develop a deeper flavor. I push the orange slice down on the mint to keep the mint from floating up.

Suggestions and Variations

During the winter months, you may also like to add a small cinnamon stick to the glass.

TOTAL PREP AND COOK TIME: 10 MINUTES • YIELD: 1 SERVING

PER SERVING: 12 CALORIES, 3 G CARBOHYDRATE (1 G FIBER, 0 G ADDED SUGARS, 2 G NET CARBS), 0 G PROTEIN, 0 G FAT, 0 MG SODIUM.

3

Satisfying Plant-Based Meals

Legumes are a big part of the Mediterranean diet, contributing all sorts of nutrients, like protein, iron, potassium, and phytonutrients. While they also contribute complex carbohydrates, fiber makes up a good portion of these carbs, which your body doesn't absorb. When legumes are balanced with non-starchy vegetables, nuts and seeds, herbs and spices, and olive oil, you get to enjoy one gorgeous plate.

EGGPLANT LASAGNA

Since this recipe makes a big pan's worth, I have the tendency to cut off a big slab and deliver to a dear friend who's had a rough or busy day. They love it.

FOR THE EGGPLANT:

2 large eggplants, trimmed, sliced ¼ inch (6 mm) thick lengthwise (about 1 ¼ pounds [568 g])

Kosher salt

Cooking oil spray

FOR THE RICOTTA FILLING:

2 eggs

1 container (16-ounce [500 g]) whole-milk ricotta cheese

1 teaspoon Italian seasoning

½ teaspoon garlic powder

¼ teaspoon salt

Freshly ground black pepper

FOR THE SAUCE:

½ teaspoon dried oregano

½ teaspoon dried basil

½ teaspoon garlic powder

¼ teaspoon salt

Freshly ground black pepper

1 (28-ounce [800 g]) can crushed tomatoes

2 cups (300 g) shredded pizza cheese, or mozzarella cheese

½ cup (50 g) grated Parmesan cheese

Preheat the oven to 350ºF (190ºC, or gas mark 4).

To make the eggplant: Place one layer of eggplant slices in a 9 × 13-inch (23 × 33 cm) baking pan and sprinkle generously with salt on both sides. Repeat with the remaining eggplant, stacking the layers. Let it sit for 15 to 20 minutes. Blot the water and salt off with a towel and move to the cutting board. Wipe out the pan. Coat the pan with cooking oil spray.

To make the filling: Whisk the eggs in a medium bowl. Add remaining filling ingredients and stir.

To make the sauce: Add the oregano, basil, garlic powder, salt, and pepper to the can of tomatoes. Stir.

In a bowl, combine the shredded cheese and Parmesan.

To assemble the lasagna, spread ½ cup (100 g) sauce in the bottom of the pan. Fit one layer of eggplant slices on top, cutting the eggplant when needed to fill large gaps. Spread 1 cup (250 g) ricotta filling in an even layer. Sprinkle with a third of the shredded cheese. Repeat with 1 cup (200 g) sauce, another layer of eggplant, and the remaining ricotta. Repeat with the remaining eggplant, sauce, and shredded cheese.

Coat a large piece of foil with cooking oil spray. Cover the pan, oil-side down. Bake until the lasagna begins to bubble around the edges and the cheese is melted in the center, about 60 minutes. Turn the oven to 425ºF (220ºC, or gas mark 7), remove the foil, and bake until lightly browned on top, about 45 minutes longer. Remove from the oven and let rest for 10 minutes before cutting.

TOTAL PREP AND COOK TIME: 2 HOURS 15 MINUTES · YIELD: 12 SERVINGS

PER SERVING: 198 CALORIES, 11 G CARBOHYDRATE (2 G FIBER, 0 G ADDED SUGARS, 9 G NET CARBS), 13 G PROTEIN, 11 G FAT, 502 MG SODIUM.

HEARTY FRENCH LENTIL STEW

This stew is so satisfying, with earthy flavors. Dried lentils require no soaking, compared to other legumes that do. French lentils have a heartier skin, and therefore hold their shape better than brown or green lentils do, but they still cook quickly in about 30 minutes. At just about ten cents per serving, lentils give you a big nutritional bang for your buck!

You may not find French lentils easily in mainstream grocery stores, but that's okay: I've made this with brown lentils—still amazing.

1 tablespoon (15 ml) extra-virgin olive oil, plus more for drizzling

1 medium carrot, diced

½ medium onion, diced

1 stalk celery, diced

2 cloves garlic, chopped

1 ¼ cups (240 g) dry French lentils (or use brown or green lentils), rinsed and drained

4 cups (940 ml) vegetable broth or chicken bone broth

2 fresh thyme sprigs

1-inch (2.5 cm) sprig fresh rosemary

2 bay leaves

½ teaspoon salt

Freshly ground black pepper

2 teaspoons sherry vinegar or apple cider vinegar

Heat a soup pot over medium heat. Add the oil. When the oil starts shimmering, add the carrot, onion, celery, and garlic. Gently sauté until tender, about 5 minutes, reducing the heat to medium-low as needed. Add the lentils, broth, thyme, rosemary, and bay leaves. Simmer until the lentils are tender to the tooth, about 30 minutes. Sprinkle in the salt and pepper and add the vinegar.

Remove the bay leaves, thyme, and rosemary. If any rosemary leaves fell off the stem, try and fetch those, too, as they can have an overpowering taste when left intact. Using an immersion blender, puree just one small section of the lentils in the pot, which thickens the stew. Ladle into wide, shallow bowls and drizzle with oil.

TOTAL PREP AND COOK TIME: 1 HOUR · YIELD: 4 SERVINGS, 1 CUP (230 G) EACH

PER SERVING: 304 CALORIES, 48 G CARBOHYDRATE (24 G FIBER, 0 G ADDED SUGARS, 24 G NET CARBS), 17 G PROTEIN, 5 G FAT, 880 MG SODIUM.

CHICKPEA VEGETABLE STEW WITH TURMERIC AND CUMIN

You probably have all of these ingredients on hand, and you can whip up this recipe in less than 30 minutes for a light lunch on a chilly day.

2 tablespoons (30 ml) extra-virgin olive oil, plus more for drizzling

1 medium carrot, diced (about ½ cup [65 g])

½ medium onion, diced (about 1 cup [160 g])

1 stalk celery, diced

2 cloves garlic, minced

½ teaspoon ground cumin

½ teaspoon ground turmeric

½ teaspoon ground ginger

¼ cup (60 ml) dry white wine

1 (15-ounce [425 g]) can chickpeas, rinsed and drained

1 (14.5-ounce [411 g]) can diced tomatoes with juice

1½ cups (355 g) vegetable broth

½ teaspoon salt

Freshly ground black pepper

Fresh herbs, coarsely chopped (like mint and Italian flat-leaf parsley)

Heat a large pot over medium heat and add the oil. When the oil begins to shimmer, add the carrot, onion, celery, and garlic. Gently sauté until tender, about 6 minutes. Stir in the cumin, turmeric, and ginger, and cook until aromatic, about 1 minute. Pour in the white wine and simmer to evaporate most of the wine, a few minutes.

Add the chickpeas, tomatoes, broth, salt, and pepper. Simmer until the flavors combine, about 10 minutes. Ladle into bowls, drizzle with more olive oil, and sprinkle with herbs.

Suggestions and Variations
For a richer taste, use coconut milk in place of broth. Or add a couple tablespoons of coconut butter, along with the broth.

TOTAL PREP AND COOK TIME: 30 MINUTES · YIELD: 4 SERVINGS, 1 GENEROUS CUP (250 G) EACH

PER SERVING: 212 CALORIES, 26 G CARBOHYDRATE (7 G FIBER, 0 G ADDED SUGARS, 19 G NET CARBS), 7 G PROTEIN, 9 G FAT, 980 MG SODIUM.

CHICKPEA FRITTERS

This recipe is essentially a simplified version of falafel made with canned chickpeas, but ready in just 20 minutes with a handful of pantry ingredients you probably have on hand. Serve with plain Greek yogurt or the Cucumber Yogurt Salad on page 44.

1 clove garlic, peeled

1 can (15-ounce [425 g]) chickpeas, rinsed and drained

1 stalk celery, cut into chunks

3 tablespoons (45 ml) extra-virgin olive oil, divided

1 lemon, zest finely grated, plus 1 tablespoon (15 ml) juice

½ teaspoon ground cumin

¼ teaspoon salt

Freshly ground black pepper

Fresh chopped chives, mint, or Italian flat-leaf parsley

Mince the garlic in the food processor. Add the chickpeas, celery, 1 tablespoon (15 ml) of the oil, lemon zest and juice, cumin, salt, and pepper. Pulse until it forms a chunky shapeable mixture, but is not smooth. Scoop into 9 balls, about 2 tablespoons (30 g) each. Squish into thick patties.

Heat a large sauté pan over medium heat. Add 1 tablespoon (15 ml) oil. When the oil is shimmering, add the patties and cook until golden, about 4 minutes. Carefully turn (the patties are on the fragile side) with a fish spatula or small flexible turner; you may need to add the remaining 1 tablespoon (15 ml) oil. Brown on the other side, another 3 to 4 minutes. Transfer to a plate lined with paper towels. Serve with a sprinkle of herbs.

TOTAL PREP AND COOK TIME: 20 MINUTES · YIELD: 3 SERVINGS, 3 PATTIES EACH

<30

PER SERVING: 205 CALORIES, 14 G CARBOHYDRATE (4 G FIBER, 0 G ADDED SUGARS, 10 G NET CARBS), 5 G PROTEIN, 15 G FAT, 461 MG SODIUM.

MEDITERRANEAN PIZZA WITH ALMOND-COCONUT FLOUR CRUST

The combination of almond flour and coconut flour make a flavorful, sturdy pizza crust. You can swap out other toppings in this, if you wish, but don't overload it with raw ingredients or you could end up with a soggy crust. In the Mediterranean, pizza toppings are kept lighter in quantity and cut thin.

FOR THE CRUST:

3 tablespoons (21 g) flaxseed meal

Water

1 cup (96 g) almond flour

¾ cup (84 g) coconut flour

1 teaspoon Italian seasoning

½ teaspoon baking powder

¼ teaspoon salt

Freshly ground black pepper

2 tablespoons (30 ml) extra-virgin olive oil

FOR THE TOPPINGS:

½ cup (112 g) pizza sauce

1 buffalo mozzarella cheese ball (8 ounces [224 g]), sliced

½ cup (35 g) paper-thin sliced mushrooms

¼ cup (25 g) Italian or Greek olives, sliced, or tiny olives left whole

Fresh basil leaves

Preheat the oven to 350°F (180°C, or gas mark 4). Tear off 2 large sheets of parchment paper to fit a pizza pan or stone.

To make the crust: Combine the flaxseed and 3 tablespoons (45 ml) of the water in a large mixing bowl. Add the almond and coconut flours on top, then the Italian seasoning, baking powder, salt, and pepper, breaking up any lumps. Add the oil and remaining ¾ cup (180 ml) water and stir until it forms a dough. Place the dough between 2 sheets of parchment paper and flatten into a large oval with a rolling pin until ⅛ inch (3 mm) thick. Carefully remove the top parchment sheet and transfer the bottom sheet with the dough to the pizza pan. Bake on the middle rack until lightly golden around the edges, about 15 minutes.

To make the toppings: Top the baked crust with the sauce, cheese, mushrooms, and olives. Bake until the cheese is melted in the middle, with a little browning around the edges, about 18 minutes. Sprinkle with basil.

TOTAL PREP AND COOK TIME: 55 MINUTES · YIELD: 6 SERVINGS, 1/6 PIZZA EACH

PER SERVING: 360 CALORIES, 16 G CARBOHYDRATE (8 G FIBER, 0 G ADDED SUGARS, 8 G NET CARBS), 15 G PROTEIN, 27 G FAT, 225 MG SODIUM,

ROASTED CAULIFLOWER STEAKS WITH RED BELL PEPPER-ALMOND SAUCE

This recipe could easily be served at any nice restaurant and will pull you out of any vegetarian food rut straight away. The romesco sauce, made of roasted red bell peppers and almonds, can also be spooned over chicken and fish.

FOR THE CAULIFLOWER:

1 small head cauliflower, stem cut off

2 tablespoons + 2 teaspoons (40 ml) extra-virgin olive oil, divided, plus more for drizzling

½ teaspoon onion powder, divided

½ teaspoon salt, divided

Freshly ground black pepper

1 medium red bell pepper

FOR THE SAUCE:

¼ cup (28 g) slivered almonds

1 tablespoon (16 g) tomato product (use what you have open, like marinara, sauce, paste, or fresh)

2 teaspoons extra-virgin olive oil

1 small clove garlic, peeled

1 teaspoon lemon juice

¼ teaspoon salt

Freshly ground black pepper

1 can (15-ounce [425 g]) chickpeas, rinsed, drained, and patted dry

Fresh coarsely chopped herbs, like basil, parsley, or green tops of scallions

¼ cup (25 g) sliced kalamata olives

Preheat the oven to 450°F (230°C, or gas mark 8) convection. Line a large baking sheet with a silicone baking mat or parchment paper.

To make the cauliflower: Slice the cauliflower into 4 thick "steaks," about 1 inch (2.5 cm) thick. Place on the prepared baking sheet. Drizzle the cauliflower with 1 tablespoon (15 ml) of the olive oil on one side, sprinkle with ¼ teaspoon of the onion powder, ¼ teaspoon of the salt, and pepper, then turn and repeat with another 1 tablespoon (15 ml) oil, the remaining ¼ teaspoon onion powder, the remaining ¼ teaspoon salt, and pepper. Place the whole red pepper on the pan and drizzle with 1 teaspoon of the oil.

Roast until the pepper is blistered and browned on all sides, about 15 minutes. Remove the pepper from the pan using tongs and place in a paper bag. Seal. Place the chickpeas on the pan and drizzle with the remaining 1 teaspoon of oil, a pinch of salt, and pepper. Turn the cauliflower. Roast until the cauliflower is browned on both sides, about 10 more minutes.

To make the sauce: After the pepper has been in the bag for at least several minutes, carefully (it will be hot and steamy!) cut out the stem and seeds. Cut the pepper into about 8 pieces. Place the pepper in a blender and add the almonds, tomato, oil, garlic, lemon juice, salt, and pepper.

To serve, place one steak on each plate. Sprinkle with the chickpeas and drizzle with the sauce. Sprinkle with the herbs and olives. Drizzle lightly with olive oil.

TOTAL PREP AND COOK TIME: 35 MINUTES · YIELD: 4 SERVINGS, 1 STEAK EACH (WITH ¼ CUP [55 G] SAUCE)

PER SERVING: 360 CALORIES, 29 G CARBOHYDRATE (10 G FIBER, 0 G ADDED SUGARS, 19 G NET CARBS), 11 G PROTEIN, 25 G FAT, 904 MG SODIUM.

VEGETARIAN MUSHROOM MEATBALLS WITH MARINARA SAUCE

You'll be amazed at how satisfying these meatless meatballs taste. My husband will eat almost any vegan dish as long as there are sautéed mushrooms in it.

2 tablespoons (30 ml) extra-virgin olive oil, divided

1 package (8-ounce [225 g]) cremini or button mushrooms, chopped fine (2¼ cups [157 g])

3 cloves garlic, 2 minced and 1 smashed

Salt and freshly ground black pepper

1 can (14-ounce [260 g]) black beans, rinsed, drained, and patted dry

1 large egg, beaten

1 tablespoon (8 g) nutritional yeast or (5 g) grated Parmesan cheese

¾ teaspoon Italian seasoning, divided

¼ teaspoon salt

1 can (14-ounce [425 g]) whole tomatoes, juice reserved

Chopped parsley, basil, or chives, for garnish (optional)

Preheat the oven to 425°F (220°C, or gas mark 7) convection. Line a large baking sheet with parchment paper.

Heat a large skillet over medium heat and add 1 tablespoon (15 ml) of the oil. Add the mushrooms and minced garlic and sauté until the liquid releases and evaporates and the mushrooms are tender, 5 to 10 minutes. Season with a pinch of salt and pepper.

Mash the beans in a medium bowl and add the egg, nutritional yeast, ½ teaspoon of the Italian seasoning, ¼ teaspoon salt, pepper, and 3 tablespoons (45 ml) juice from the tomatoes. Add the cooked mushrooms and stir well. Scoop into 1-inch (2.5 cm) balls and place on the prepared baking sheet. You should get 9 balls. Drizzle with the remaining 1 tablespoon (15 ml) oil. Bake until golden, 12 to 15 minutes.

While the beanballs bake, squeeze the tomatoes into the skillet (no need to wash it), using clean hands. Add ¼ cup (60 ml) of the reserved tomato juice, the smashed garlic clove, remaining ¼ teaspoon Italian seasoning, and a pinch of salt and pepper.

To serve, plate the beanballs and spoon over the sauce. Garnish with chopped fresh herbs if you have some on hand, like parsley, basil, or chives.

TOTAL PREP AND COOK TIME: 40 MINUTES · YIELD: 3 SERVINGS, 3 BALLS EACH (WITH SAUCE)

PER SERVING: 270 CALORIES, 31 G CARBOHYDRATE (11 G FIBER, 0 G ADDED SUGARS, 20 G NET CARBS), 14 G PROTEIN, 11 G FAT, 183 MG SODIUM.

SLOW COOKER WHITE BEAN STEW WITH TOMATOES AND SWISS CHARD

Just toss all of these ingredients into your slow cooker and go, and you get to come home to a comforting bowl later.

1 can (15-ounce [425 g]) cannellini beans, rinsed and drained

1 can (14.5-ounce [411 g]) diced tomatoes in juice

1 bunch Swiss chard, chopped

2 cups (470 ml) vegetable broth

½ medium onion, diced (about 1 cup [160 g])

1 teaspoon Italian seasoning

1 clove garlic, smashed with wide side of knife

2 teaspoons liquid aminos or soy sauce

1 tablespoon (8 g) nutritional yeast

¼ teaspoon salt

Freshly ground black pepper

1 teaspoon apple cider vinegar

Combine all of the ingredients in a slow cooker. Cover and cook on low for 2 to 3 hours.

TOTAL PREP AND COOK TIME: 3 HOURS · YIELD: 4 SERVINGS, 1½ CUPS (450 G) EACH

PER SERVING: 182 CALORIES, 35 G CARBOHYDRATE (9 G FIBER, 0 G ADDED SUGARS, 26 G NET CARBS), 11 G PROTEIN, 1 G FAT, 1091 MG SODIUM.

CHICKPEA PANCAKES WITH MUSHROOMS AND KALE

Well-known in the Provençal region of France, chickpea pancakes *(socca)* are a delicious and satisfying vegan snack. I make them a meal by piling on mushrooms and kale.

FOR THE CHICKPEA PANCAKES:

½ cup (45 g) chickpea flour

½ cup (120 ml) unsweetened milk (animal or plant-based), broth, or water

4 tablespoons (60 ml) extra-virgin olive oil, divided

Pinch of salt

FOR THE VEGETABLES:

8 ounces (225 g) shiitake mushrooms, stems removed

2 tablespoons (30 ml) extra-virgin olive oil, divided

3 fresh thyme sprigs

¼ teaspoon salt, divided

Freshly ground black pepper

1 bunch kale, ribs removed, leaves chopped into bite-size pieces

To make the pancakes: In a medium-size bowl, whisk together the flour, milk, 2 tablespoons (30 ml) of the oil, and salt until only tiny lumps remain. Let it sit for at least 15 minutes while you cut the vegetables.

To make the vegetables: Quarter the larger mushrooms, halve the medium-size mushrooms, and leave the small mushrooms whole. Heat a 10-inch (25 cm) sauté pan over medium heat. Add 1 table-spoon (15 ml) of the oil, the mushrooms, thyme sprigs, ⅛ teaspoon of the salt, and pepper. Brown the mushrooms for about 5 minutes. Transfer to a plate.

Put the pan back on the heat and add the remaining 1 tablespoon (15 ml) oil, the kale, remaining ⅛ teaspoon salt, and pepper. Sauté while turning frequently with tongs until tender, about 5 minutes. Transfer to a plate.

To cook the pancakes: Scrape any bits of vegetables from the pan. Heat the pan over medium-high heat. Add 1 tablespoon (15 ml) oil and when it is shimmering, add half of the batter, about ½ cup (50 g), to form a thin pancake about 6 inches (15 cm) wide. Reduce the heat to medium and brown on one side, 2 to 3 minutes. Flip and cook on the other side, about 2 minutes. Remove from the pan and repeat with the remaining batter and the remaining 1 tablespoon (15 ml) oil.

Plate the pancakes and top with the kale and mushrooms.

TOTAL PREP AND COOK TIME: 40 MINUTES · YIELD: 2 SERVINGS, 1 PANCAKE EACH (WITH KALE AND MUSHROOMS)

PER SERVING: 530 CALORIES, 26 G CARBOHYDRATE (10 G FIBER, 0 G ADDED SUGARS, 16 G NET CARBS), 11 G PROTEIN, 45 G FAT, 490 MG SODIUM.

SHEET PAN CHICKPEA AND BROCCOLI DINNER

"You should make this for people," my husband announced after eating my rendition of this dish. It's easy to swap out different vegetables for whatever you have on hand, too. The inspiration for this comes from a burrito recipe on the blog Bad Manners that I have made many, many times, and with a variety of vegetable swaps depending on what I have on hand. My version here offers a Mediterranean flavor profile. My husband and I love them all.

1 can (15-ounce [425 g]) chickpeas, rinsed and drained

1 small broccoli crown, chopped to the size of the chickpeas

1 package (8-ounce [225 g]) mushrooms, chopped

1 red bell pepper, diced

½ medium onion, diced

2 cloves garlic, minced

2 tablespoons (30 ml) liquid aminos or soy sauce

½ teaspoon smoked or sweet paprika

½ teaspoon ground coriander

⅛ teaspoon crushed red pepper flakes (or more if you like it spicy)

Freshly ground black pepper

2 tablespoons (30 ml) extra-virgin olive oil

Juice of ½ lemon (about 1 tablespoon [15 ml])

¼ cup (15 g) parsley leaves, coarsely chopped

Diced avocado

Preheat the oven to 425°F (220°C, or gas mark 6) convection.

Place the chickpeas, broccoli, mushrooms, red pepper, onion, garlic, liquid aminos, paprika, coriander, red pepper flakes, black pepper, and oil in a large bowl. Toss to coat everything evenly. Spread on a large baking sheet. Bake for 20 minutes. Toss with two spatulas. Bake until the broccoli begins to brown, about 10 more minutes. Drizzle with the lemon juice and sprinkle with the parsley. Toss again.

Spoon into shallow bowls and top with the diced avocado.

Suggestions and Variations
• If you don't have a bell pepper on hand, I've swapped that with a large diced carrot—delish.

TOTAL PREP AND COOK TIME: 1 HOUR · YIELD: 4 SERVINGS

PER SERVING: 183 CALORIES, 22 G CARBOHYDRATE (6 G FIBER, 0 G ADDED SUGARS, 16 G NET CARBS), 8 G PROTEIN, 9 G FAT, 730 MG SODIUM.

LIMA BEAN CASSOULET WITH ZUCCHINI AND BUTTERNUT SQUASH

This dish offers a variety of textures, tastes, and colors and I love it for a vegetarian dinner. I also gave my friend some to try, with no explanation on what to do with it, and she loved it cold as a salad for lunch!

With vegetables, beans, and cheese, it comes together as an all-in-one meal, so you can enjoy a generous serving. A ½ cup (38 g) of lima beans gives you just 110 calories, with 6 grams protein, 7 grams fiber, 13 grams net carbs, and 10 percent of the Daily Value for iron.

Cooking oil spray

1 small (1 pound [455 g]) butternut squash

2 cups (150 g) frozen lima beans, thawed

1 medium zucchini, diced

¼ medium red onion, diced

1 can (8-ounce [225 g]) tomato sauce

1 tablespoon (15 ml) extra-virgin olive oil, plus more for drizzling

1 tablespoon (8 g) nutritional yeast

1 tablespoon (15 ml) lemon juice

1 clove garlic, minced

1 teaspoon dried oregano

½ teaspoon salt

Freshly ground black pepper

4 ounces (115 g) soft goat cheese

Fresh Italian flat-leaf parsley, coarsely chopped

Preheat the oven to 375°F (190°C, or gas mark 5). Coat four individual ramekins or a 9 × 9-inch (23 × 23 cm) baking dish with cooking oil spray.

Trim the ends off the squash. Cut in half lengthwise. Scoop out the seeds. Prick the skin all over with a fork and microwave for 1 minute. Peel. Dice into ¼-inch (6 mm) cubes.

In a large mixing bowl, combine the squash, lima beans, zucchini, onion, tomato sauce, oil, nutritional yeast, lemon juice, garlic, oregano, salt, and pepper. Mix well to combine. Crumble in the goat cheese and stir gently. Pour the ingredients into the baking dish or ramekins and cover with foil. Bake until you hear and see bubbling all around the edges and the squash is fork tender, about 30-40 minutes. Sprinkle with the parsley and drizzle with more olive oil.

TOTAL PREP AND COOK TIME: 1 HOUR · YIELD: 6 SERVINGS

PER SERVING: 176 CALORIES, 22 G CARBOHYDRATE (5 G FIBER, 0 G ADDED SUGARS, 17 G NET CARBS), 9 G PROTEIN, 7 G FAT, 295 MG SODIUM.

CREAMY BELUGA LENTILS WITH GINGER AND GARLIC

Beluga lentils are pretty wild, in a variety of aspects, and I love them for it. With a spherical shape, poppy texture, and midnight black color, they resemble beluga caviar. They have a luxurious taste and texture, yet you're still eating good ol', healthy, plant-based beans!

¾ cup (144 g) dried beluga lentils

¾ cup (120 g) diced onion

2 cloves garlic, peeled and whole

1 bay leaf

2 tablespoons (32 g) tomato paste

1 tablespoon (8 g) grated gingerroot

1 teaspoon chili powder

¼ teaspoon salt

Freshly ground black pepper

½ cup (115 g) plain whole-milk Greek yogurt

2 tablespoons (30 ml) extra-virgin olive oil

½ cup (8 g) cilantro leaves

Rinse the lentils, removing any broken lentils or foreign debris. Drain. Place in a pot and cover with 1 inch (2.5 cm) water. Add the onion, garlic, and bay leaf. Bring to a boil, then reduce the heat and simmer until the lentils are tender, about 30 minutes. Remove the garlic and bay leaf.

Add the tomato paste, ginger, chili powder, salt, and pepper. Stir and bring to a simmer. Turn off the heat. Spoon into bowls. Dollop each serving with yogurt. Drizzle with the olive oil and serve with the cilantro.

Suggestions and Variations
I love to serve this with stir-fried cauliflower "rice" and a mango and red onion salad with a squeeze of lime juice.

TOTAL PREP AND COOK TIME: 40 MINUTES · YIELD: 3 SERVINGS, 1 CUP (170 G) EACH

PER SERVING: 193 CALORIES, 16 G CARBOHYDRATE (3 G FIBER, 0 G ADDED SUGARS, 13 G NET CARBS), 8 G PROTEIN, 11 G FAT, 362 MG SODIUM.

EASY ASPARAGUS FRITTATA

While a frittata sounds brunchy and fancy, it is seriously so easy, you'll want to make it on the regular. It's really versatile; from breakfast to lunch to dinner, it can be savored anytime during the day. It's also a wonderful way to use up any vegetable bits you have in the fridge, whether they are leftovers or raw.

6 large eggs

¼ cup (60 ml) milk

¼ cup (25 g) grated Parmesan cheese

¼ + ⅛ teaspoon salt

Freshly ground black pepper

½ bunch asparagus

1 tablespoon (15 ml) extra-virgin olive oil

½ cup (80 g) diced red onion

Whisk the eggs, milk, Parmesan, salt, and pepper in a bowl. Break off the woody bottom third or fourth from the asparagus and discard. Slice the stalks of the asparagus into small pieces, reserving the top 1 to 2 inches (2.5 to 5 cm) of the tips.

Heat a medium sauté pan, about 10 inches (25 cm), over medium heat. Add the oil. When the oil is shimmering, add the onions and asparagus. Sauté until the onions are translucent. Pour in the eggs. Cover and cook over medium-low heat for about 10 minutes.

Suggestions and Variations
- You can substitute the asparagus with other vegetables like broccoli, zucchini, and mushrooms. If the vegetables are already cooked, you can add them in toward the end of cooking the onion.
- Red onion can be substituted with any type of onion, like white or yellow onion, leeks, or scallions.

Make It for the Whole Family
For your picky eaters, it's not too difficult to push all of the greenery in a couple of servings out of the frittata, before you add the egg, gently pouring it into the blank space.

<30 **TOTAL PREP AND COOK TIME: 30 MINUTES · YIELD: 6 SERVINGS, 1 SLICE EACH**

PER SERVING: 127 CALORIES, 4 G CARBOHYDRATE (1 G FIBER, 0 G ADDED SUGARS, 3 G NET CARBS), 9 G PROTEIN, 9 G FAT, 297 MG SODIUM.

30-MINUTE PANTRY SHAKSHUKA

Before being a darling of social media food pics, *shakshuka* has existed in Mediterranean cuisine for centuries in a variety of shapes and forms, depending on the country.

While it may sound exotic, rest assured you probably have nearly everything you need in your fridge and pantry to prepare this dish.

2 tablespoons (30 ml) extra-virgin olive oil, plus more for drizzling

½ medium onion, diced (about 1 cup [160 g])

1 clove garlic, minced

1 tablespoon (7 g) sweet paprika, plus more for garnish

2 teaspoons ground cumin

1 ½ teaspoons ground coriander

¼ teaspoon ground nutmeg

⅛ teaspoon ground cayenne

Freshly ground black pepper

1 can (28-ounce [793 g]) whole tomatoes

½ teaspoon salt

8 large eggs

1 ¼ cups (75 g or 20 g) fresh parsley or cilantro leaves, coarsely chopped

Place a large skillet over medium heat. Add the oil. When the oil is shimmering, add the onion and garlic, reducing the heat to low. Gently sauté until the onions are translucent, about 5 minutes. Sprinkle in the paprika, cumin, coriander, nutmeg, cayenne, and pepper and toast until aromatic, about 1 minute. Stir in the tomatoes and salt. Gently pierce each tomato with a wooden spoon before breaking them into smaller bits so they don't squirt all over you and your kitchen.

Decide how many eggs will be eaten in this sitting. Carve out that number of wells in the sauce to make room for simmering the eggs. Crack each egg and add one to each well. Cover with a lid or foil and simmer over medium-low heat until the whites are cooked but the yolks are still runny, about 4 minutes. Turn off the heat and sprinkle the eggs with more paprika and pepper.

Using a large serving spoon, scoop the eggs with sauce, one at a time, into shallow bowls. Drizzle with olive oil and sprinkle with parsley.

Recipe Note
This sauce tastes even better the next day and the day after that! Save any leftover sauce and reheat in a smaller pan, cooking a fresh batch of eggs.

TOTAL PREP AND COOK TIME: 30 MINUTES · YIELD: 4 SERVINGS, 2 EGGS EACH (WITH SAUCE)

PER SERVING: 245 CALORIES, 13 G CARBOHYDRATE (6 G FIBER, 0 G ADDED SUGARS, 7 G NET CARBS), 15 G PROTEIN, 16 G FAT, 664 MG SODIUM.

ALMOND FLOUR PUMPKIN PANCAKES

If you're jonesing for pancakes, these will fit the bill for you. They are fluffy and moist, orange-hued, and warming from the spices.

¼ cup (24 g) almond flour

¼ cup (30 g) coconut flour

1 teaspoon baking powder

½ teaspoon pumpkin pie spice (or use
   ¼ teaspoon each cinnamon and ginger)

3 large eggs

½ cup (115 g) canned 100% pumpkin

¼ cup (60 ml) milk

1 teaspoon vanilla extract

2 teaspoons neutral oil, like avocado oil

Whisk the flours, baking powder, and spices in a mixing bowl. Add the eggs, pumpkin, milk, and vanilla. Stir until completely combined.

Heat a griddle or large skillet over medium heat. Drizzle with the oil. When the oil is shimmering, drop the batter onto the pan using a ¼-cup (60 g) scoop. Reduce the heat to medium-low. Cook until golden on one side, about 4 minutes. Carefully but swiftly flip the pancakes using a spatula. Brown on the other side, 2 to 3 minutes.

Suggestions and Variations
I love to top these pancakes with:
• Buttery spread and just the *slightest* drizzle of real maple syrup
• Applesauce made with no added sugar (pureed roasted apples taste so good)

TOTAL PREP AND COOK TIME: 15 MINUTES · YIELD: 3 SERVINGS, 2 PANCAKES EACH

PER SERVING: 209 CALORIES, 12 G CARBOHYDRATE (6 G FIBER, 0 G ADDED SUGARS, 6 G NET CARBS), 11 G PROTEIN, 14 G FAT, 84 MG SODIUM.

4

Succulent
Seafood

Seafood dishes of the Mediterranean are so fresh and light. If you are preparing fresh seafood, you can't really mess up the recipe unless you overcook it. Trust me—I will hold your hand through this. The beauty of these dishes is that most of them are ready in 30 minutes or less. If you can't find the seafood listed in the title, I aimed to include substitutions wherever possible. Opt for what is fresh and available in your market.

SEAFOOD STEW WITH TOMATOES AND WHITE WINE

Known as *bouillabaisse* in French and *cioppino* in Italian, in Indiana where I live they just call it good ol' seafood stew! I've enjoyed the dish in all three locations, and then some. Be sure to follow these two important steps:

First, build depth of flavor in the broth; otherwise, it just tastes like tomato juice. I sauté the shrimp shells (the smell is glorious) and simmer them in bottled clam juice and chicken broth for 15 minutes. If you have an extra 15 to 30 minutes, simmer that much longer.

Second, add the seafood during the last few minutes, so you end up with moist, tender seafood, not rubber balls.

1 pound (455 g) in-shell medium-large shrimp, thawed

1 tablespoon (15 ml) extra-virgin olive oil, plus more for drizzling

½ teaspoon crushed red pepper flakes

1 clove garlic, thinly sliced

½ cup (120 ml) dry white wine, like Sauvignon Blanc or Chardonnay

3 bottles (8-ounce [236 ml]) clam juice

¼ teaspoon dried thyme

1 bay leaf

¼ cup (15 g) coarsely chopped Italian flat-leaf parsley, plus 2 whole stems, divided

2 cups (235 ml) chicken bone broth

1 can (14.5-ounce [411 g]) diced tomatoes

¼ teaspoon salt

½ pound (227 g) whitefish, like perch, tilapia, or pollock, cut into 2-inch (5 cm) pieces

½ lemon, visible seeds removed

Peel the shrimp and reserve the shells, including the tails. In a soup pot, heat the oil over medium heat. When the oil is shimmering, add the shells, red pepper flakes, and garlic. Gently sauté until the shells are aromatic and the garlic is golden, about 5 minutes. Pour in the white wine and simmer until nearly evaporated, about 2 minutes. Add the clam juice, thyme, bay leaf, and 2 parsley stems, and simmer for 15 to 30 minutes, depending on how much time you have. Reduce the heat as needed to maintain gentle bubbling. With a slotted spoon or spider strainer, remove the shells, bay leaf, and parsley stems.

Add the chicken broth, tomatoes, and salt. Bring to a simmer. Add the shrimp and whitefish, pushing it into the liquid to cover completely. Cover, maintaining the heat on low, and set a timer for 3 minutes. The seafood will be opaque white in the middle when done. Turn off the heat. Squeeze in the juice of the lemon half. Ladle the stew into bowls, drizzle with olive oil, and sprinkle with the chopped parsley.

Suggestions and Variations
To veg things up, line the bowl with baby arugula and ladle the piping-hot soup on top.

TOTAL PREP AND COOK TIME: 1 HOUR · YIELD: 4 SERVINGS, ABOUT 1 ¾ CUPS (425 ML) EACH

PER SERVING: 158 CALORIES, 7 G CARBOHYDRATE (1 G FIBER, 0 G ADDED SUGARS, 6 G NET CARBS), 29 G PROTEIN, 6 G FAT, 850 MG SODIUM.

SAUTÉED TILAPIA PROVENÇAL

This dish reminds me of countless meals I've enjoyed in the Mediterranean: light, delicious, fresh, seafood-y, and tomatoey. It's ready in 30 minutes and cooked on your stovetop. While tilapia isn't exactly Mediterranean, it is similar to so many European whitefish and is easy to find fresh in the U.S. Just opt for those from the U.S., Mexico, Indonesia, or Argentina, which has the cleanest ponds, or from big lakes. Avoid tilapia from Thailand and China. Or substitute with another whitefish like flounder.

1 pound (455 g) tilapia fillets

½ teaspoon salt, divided

Freshly ground black pepper

½ cup (50 g) almond flour or meal

2 tablespoons (30 ml) extra-virgin olive oil, plus more for drizzling, divided

1 or 2 cloves garlic, peeled and quartered

1 container (8-ounce [225 g]) mushrooms, quartered

2 medium tomatoes, chopped (or 1½ cups [270 g] halved cherry tomatoes)

3 tablespoons (45 ml) dry white wine

¼ cup (25 g) olives, sliced or filleted

Fresh tiny basil leaves or coarsely chopped Italian flat-leaf parsley

Lemon wedges

Season the tilapia with ¼ teaspoon of the salt and some pepper, then coat in the almond flour. Heat a large sauté pan or skillet over medium-high heat. Add 1 tablespoon (15 ml) of the oil. When the oil is shimmering, add the tilapia. Cook until browned on one side and cooked nearly halfway through, about 4 minutes. Turn and cook through, about 2 minutes. Transfer the tilapia to a plate and scrape out any almond flour bits from the pan.

Put the pan back on the heat and add the remaining 1 tablespoon (15 ml) oil. Add the garlic and mushrooms. Sauté until tender, about 5 minutes. Add the tomatoes and wine and simmer over medium heat until the tomatoes are softened, about 3 minutes. Stir in the olives, remaining ¼ teaspoon salt, and pepper.

Plate the tilapia and spoon the tomatoes crosswise across the tilapia. Drizzle with olive oil and sprinkle with herbs. Serve with lemon wedges.

Make It for the Whole Family
For my kids, I cut the tilapia into finger-like shapes and serve it with their favorite dip.

 TOTAL PREP AND COOK TIME: 30 MINUTES · YIELD: 4 SERVINGS

PER SERVING: 305 CALORIES, 9 G CARBOHYDRATE (3 G FIBER, 0 G ADDED SUGARS, 6 G NET CARBS), 28 G PROTEIN, 17 G FAT, 577 MG SODIUM.

SHRIMP PAELLA WITH CAULIFLOWER "RICE"

Chances are that you've eaten Valencian-style paella, a rather fluffy rice dish with yellow-hued rice. The paella that holds a special place in my heart, however, is the one commonly found in Barcelona, Spain, with a deep red color from tomatoes and chiles and more reminiscent of the style I make this dish.

1 pound (455 g) peeled, deveined medium-size shrimp (about 20 count size), tails on

2 tablespoons (30 ml) extra-virgin olive oil, divided

2½ cups (812 g) cauliflower "rice" (See Recipe Note on page 129)

1 cup (150 g) diced red bell pepper

2 cloves garlic, minced

¼ teaspoon + ⅛ teaspoon salt, divided

Freshly ground black pepper

3 tablespoons (48 g) tomato paste

1 teaspoon smoked paprika

1 teaspoon chili powder (or other mild ground chile)

1½ cups (352 ml) clam broth or chicken bone broth, divided

2 teaspoons arrowroot powder

¼ cup (15 g) chopped fresh Italian flat-leaf parsley

Lemon wedges

Heat a large sauté pan or paella pan over medium-high heat. Pat the shrimp dry. Add 1 tablespoon (15 ml) of the oil to the pan. When the oil is shimmering, add the shrimp and brown undisturbed, about 3 minutes. Turn the shrimp to the other side and brown. Transfer the shrimp to a plate.

Reduce the heat to medium. Add the remaining 1 tablespoon (15 ml) oil. Add the cauliflower, bell pepper, and garlic. Sprinkle with ¼ teaspoon of the salt and pepper. Sauté for about 5 minutes, scraping up any browned bits from the bottom of the pan as the water releases from the vegetables. Add the tomato paste and stir. Add the paprika and chili powder to a dry area of the pan and toast for about 1 minute. Pour in 1¼ cups (295 ml) of the broth. Add the shrimp back in, pushing it gently into the broth. Sprinkle on the remaining ⅛ teaspoon salt. Simmer until the shrimp is cooked through and the vegetables are tender, about 5 minutes.

Whisk the arrowroot into the remaining ¼ cup (60 ml) broth, then drizzle all over the cauliflower, shaking the pan gently back and forth.

Sprinkle on the parsley and spritz with lemon juice.

Recipe Note
If you have some saffron on hand, by all means, add a pinch when you add the broth.

TOTAL PREP AND COOK TIME: 30 MINUTES · YIELD: 4 SERVINGS

PER SERVING: 197 CALORIES, 9 G CARBOHYDRATE (3 G FIBER, 0 G ADDED SUGARS, 6 G NET CARBS), 25 G PROTEIN, 8 G FAT, 465 MG SODIUM.

Clean Eating Kitchen: The Low-Carb Mediterranean Cookbook

BAKED SALMON WITH PARSLEY AND GARLIC CRUST

I cook fresh salmon often during peak salmon season, which is during the summer months. The addition of herbs and lemon accents the fish nicely, without overpowering it.

¼ cup (15 g) coarsely chopped parsley leaves

1 lemon, zest finely grated, then fruit cut into wedges

1 tablespoon (11 g) Dijon mustard

1 clove garlic, minced

1 tablespoon (15 ml) extra-virgin olive oil

1 pound (455 g) salmon fillet

¼ teaspoon salt

Freshly ground black pepper

Preheat the oven to 350°F (180°C, or gas mark 3). Line a baking sheet with parchment or use a silicone baking mat or baking dish.

Combine the parsley, lemon zest, Dijon, garlic, and olive oil in a small bowl.

Place the salmon on the prepared baking sheet. Season the salmon all over with salt and pepper. Spoon the parsley mixture on top of the salmon. Bake until it's sizzling around the edges and medium in the center, before it becomes firm, about 20 minutes. The exact time will depend on the thickness of the salmon, and if you are baking individual portions of salmon, it will cook in about 15–20 minutes.

Suggestions and Variations
If you keep an herb garden in the summer and have a range of varieties like chives, basil, and dill, feel free to mix those in with the parsley.

Make It for the Whole Family
Your kids might appreciate small nuggets of salmon, simply seasoned with just salt. These pieces will cook quicker, in about 10 minutes.

TOTAL PREP AND COOK TIME: 30 MINUTES · YIELD: 4 SERVINGS

<30 PER SERVING: 182 CALORIES, 1 G CARBOHYDRATE (0 G FIBER, 0 G ADDED SUGARS, 1 G NET CARBS), 24 G PROTEIN, 9 G FAT, 322 MG SODIUM.

SAUTÉED SALMON WITH FIGS

While this recipe may *look* kind of fancy, I assure you, it is so easy to prepare! If you've never eaten or cooked with figs (don't worry, you're not alone), it's pretty easy, since there's not too much you have to do with them except snip the stem. My favorite salmon to use for searing like this is fresh king salmon, which is moist and tender.

1 teaspoon ground coriander

½ teaspoon ground cinnamon

¼ teaspoon salt

Freshly ground black pepper

1 pound (455 g) salmon fillet,
   cut into 4 pieces

1 tablespoon (15 ml) extra-virgin
   olive oil

2 scallions, thinly sliced, white
   and green parts separated

½ cup (75 g) dried figs, quartered
   (about 6 figs)

½ cup (120 ml) chicken bone broth

1 teaspoon sherry vinegar or
   red wine vinegar

Combine the coriander, cinnamon, salt, and pepper in a small bowl. Sprinkle the seasoning on all sides of the salmon. Heat a large sauté pan over medium heat. Add the oil. When the oil is shimmering, add the salmon. Cover and brown on one side, about 4 minutes. Then turn and cook until cooked through, about 3 minutes, depending on thickness. Turn off the heat and transfer the salmon to a plate.

Carefully (the pan will be hot) wipe the excess oil out the pan with an adequate amount of scrunched-up paper towel. Place the pan back over medium heat. Add the white parts of the scallions and sauté for about 1 minute. Add the figs and broth and simmer until the broth reduces by half, about 4 minutes. Stir in the vinegar.

To serve, spoon the fig sauce onto plates and place the salmon on top. Sprinkle with the green parts of the scallions.

Nutrition Note

Figs are naturally part of the Mediterranean diet and offer a wealth of nutrients, including being an excellent source of fiber, plus phytonutrients, potassium, and some calcium. One fig contains about 25 calories and about 5 grams net carbs with no added sugar, satisfying your sweet tooth.

Suggestions and Variations

Take advantage of fresh fig season from May to December. To prepare this recipe with fresh figs, sauté the figs for a couple of minutes, remove them from the pan, and then add the broth.

TOTAL PREP AND COOK TIME: 25 MINUTES · YIELD: 4 SERVINGS

PER SERVING: 298 CALORIES, 13 G CARBOHYDRATE (2 G FIBER, 0 G ADDED SUGARS, 11 G NET CARBS), 25 G PROTEIN, 17 G FAT, 215 MG SODIUM.

LEMON BAKED COD WITH PISTACHIO CRUST

This 30-minute recipe is light and satisfying, offering a nice crunch from the pistachios. This flavor profile would also work great on other seafoods available, like salmon, trout, and tilapia.

3 tablespoons (45 ml) extra-virgin olive oil

1 lemon, zest finely grated, then fruit cut into wedges

1 teaspoon Italian seasoning

¼ teaspoon salt

Freshly ground black pepper

1 pound (455 g) cod or pollock fillet, cut into 4 pieces

⅓ cup (37 g) roasted and salted shelled pistachios, finely chopped

Preheat the oven to 350ºF (180ºC, or gas mark 4). Line a baking sheet with parchment paper or a silicone baking mat.

In a small bowl, combine the olive oil, lemon zest, Italian seasoning, salt, and pepper. Place the cod on the prepared baking sheet and spoon the seasoned oil on the fillet, rubbing it onto all sides. Dip the tops of the cod into the pistachios and press gently, forming a top crust, and place back on the pan. Bake until the fish is sizzling around the edges and opaque and nearly firm in the middle, about 15 minutes. Serve with the lemon wedges.

Suggestions and Variations

My husband's *must-have* accompaniment with most seafood dishes is tartar sauce. And his is *the* best! He makes it quickly with just a handful of ingredients: mayonnaise, chopped dill pickles, lemon juice, Cajun seasoning, Dijon mustard, salt, and pepper. While it isn't required to make this dish, it is a nice addition if tartar sauce is a must for you, too.

Make It for the Whole Family

Your kids may be more inclined to try simple fish fingers. Cut up one of the fillets into strips and season with salt and pepper. You can bake them on the same pan, but they may cook a little faster than the other portions.

 TOTAL PREP AND COOK TIME: 30 MINUTES · YIELD: 4 SERVINGS

PER SERVING: 220 CALORIES, 3 G CARBOHYDRATE (1 G FIBER, 0 G ADDED SUGARS, 2 G NET CARBS), 19 G PROTEIN, 15 G FAT, 489 MG SODIUM.

BROILED FLOUNDER WITH LEMON, PARSLEY, AND GARLIC

Flounder is a whitefish similar to halibut in taste and texture, but in smaller fillets. The term *flounder* is a general term for flatfish species such as fluke, dab, and lemon sole. This is a standby recipe in my rotation, since it is so easy to make with any type of whitefish and staple ingredients I always have on hand. While you may not see flounder everywhere in fresh fish cases, you may find it in the freezer section in common grocery stores. You may also substitute with tilapia, but since tilapia fillets can be quite large, increase the cooking time as needed.

Cooking oil spray

1 pound (455 g) flounder* fillets (about 4 fillets), patted dry

1 tablespoon (15 ml) extra-virgin olive oil, plus more for drizzling

1 lemon, zest finely grated, then fruit cut into wedges

1 clove garlic, sliced

¼ teaspoon salt

Freshly ground black pepper

¼ cup (15 g) coarsely chopped Italian flat-leaf parsley

1 teaspoon capers, chopped (optional)

Move an oven rack to 6 inches (15 cm) below the broiler. Preheat the oven to low broil. Line a baking sheet with foil for easier cleanup. Coat the foil with oil spray.

Place the fish on the prepared baking sheet. In a small bowl, combine the oil, lemon zest, garlic, salt, and pepper and spread on top of the fish. Broil until the edges are sizzling and the centers are opaque white, about 10 minutes, though cooking time will vary depending on the thickness of the fillets.

Sprinkle with the parsley and capers and serve with the lemon wedges. Drizzle with additional oil, if desired.

Make It for the Whole Family
*On nights I cook whitefish prepared with a variety of ingredients, I always reserve a fillet for my kids that I cut up into finger-size pieces and simply season with salt. I cook it on the same pan as the other fish, but perhaps in a little foil "boat" to keep it away from other flavors.

TOTAL PREP AND COOK TIME: 25 MINUTES · YIELD: 4 SERVINGS

PER SERVING: 151 CALORIES, 1 G CARBOHYDRATE (0 G FIBER, 0 G ADDED SUGARS, 1 G NET CARBS), 16 G PROTEIN, 9 G FAT, 456 MG SODIUM.

SHRIMP AND ZOODLES WITH FRESH TOMATO SAUCE

The key to making fresh tomato sauce is using perfectly ripe tomatoes and good olive oil. Never store whole tomatoes in the refrigerator. If your tomatoes aren't fully ready, ripen them on the windowsill, checking on them each day. I usually buy vine-on tomatoes, which tend to be closer to ripe and more flavorful.

FOR THE ZOODLES:

1 tablespoon (15 ml) extra-virgin olive oil

2 cloves garlic, smashed with wide side of knife

4 small zucchini, spiralized (about 6 cups [678 g]), chopped through once to shorten strands

¼ teaspoon salt

Freshly ground black pepper

FOR THE SHRIMP AND TOMATO SAUCE:

¼ cup (60 ml) extra-virgin olive oil, divided, plus more for drizzling

1 pound (455 g) medium shrimp, peeled, deveined, and tails removed

Pinch plus ½ teaspoon salt, divided

Freshly ground black pepper

2 cloves garlic, smashed with wide side of knife

1 pound (455 g) stem-on cocktail-size tomatoes, quartered

Finely grated Parmesan cheese

1 cup (40 g) fresh basil leaves, coarsely chopped, tiny leaves reserved for garnish

To make the zoodles: Heat a large skillet over medium-low heat and add the 1 tablespoon (15 ml) oil. When the oil is shimmering, add the garlic and sauté until aromatic, about 1 minute. Add the zoodles and sauté until they're tender enough to twirl around a fork like spaghetti and are bright green, about 5 minutes. Season with the salt and pepper.

To make the shrimp and tomato sauce: Place the skillet over medium heat. Add 2 tablespoons (30 ml) of the oil. When the oil is shimmering, add the shrimp. Cook on one side until opaque about halfway through, about 5 minutes. Turn the shrimp and cook through, about 2 minutes. Season with a pinch of salt and pepper. Transfer to a plate.

Place the pan back over medium heat. Add the remaining 2 tablespoons (30 ml) oil and the garlic. When the oil is shimmering, add the tomatoes, remaining ½ teaspoon salt, and pepper. Simmer until the tomatoes soften, but are still chunky, about 9 minutes. Stir in the basil.

Add the cooked zoodles and shrimp to the sauce and combine using tongs.

Portion into bowls and sprinkle with the Parmesan and tiny basil leaves. Drizzle with additional olive oil, if desired.

TOTAL PREP AND COOK TIME: 60 MINUTES · YIELD: 4 SERVINGS, 1 ½ CUPS (170 G) EACH

PER SERVING: 281 CALORIES, 11 G CARBOHYDRATE (3 G FIBER, 0 G ADDED SUGARS, 8 G NET CARBS), 21 G PROTEIN, 18 G FAT, 594 MG SODIUM.

MEDITERRANEAN GRILLED SHRIMP

While vacationing in Rovinj, Croatia, one of our most memorable meals was the simplest dish—fresh whole shrimp grilled in the shells. They were just bursting with juicy flavors of the sea. Since whole fresh shrimp isn't easy to come by, unless you live on the coast, I created this recipe using the kind you typically find with just the tails, but buy those with the shells on, which adds more shrimp flavor and keeps the shrimp moist. Marinate the shrimp first so the flavors seep beyond the shell.

1 pound (455 g) large in-shell shrimp, fresh or thawed (10/15 count size)

Fresh thyme sprigs

3 cloves garlic, smashed with wide side of knife

2 tablespoons (30 ml) extra-virgin olive oil

1 lemon, zest finely grated, then fruit cut into wedges

¼ teaspoon salt

Freshly ground black pepper

Blot the shrimp dry. Cut the shrimp the long way through the backs, about halfway through the meat. Place the shrimp in a shallow dish. Add the thyme and garlic, drizzle with the oil, and sprinkle on the lemon zest. Marinate for at least 30 minutes, up to a few hours.

When ready to cook the shrimp, preheat the grill to medium heat, about 350-400°F (180-200°C). Pull the shrimp from the fridge to allow them to temper. Sprinkle the shrimp with salt and pepper. Grill the shrimp until opaque nearly halfway through, a few minutes. Turn and cook through, a couple minutes more. Remove and spritz on lemon juice.

Suggestions and Variations
To change up the flavors, try using an orange in place of the lemon, and other fresh herbs in place of thyme, like basil, chives, or dill.

TOTAL PREP AND COOK TIME: 30 MINUTES, PLUS MARINATING · YIELD: 4 SERVINGS, ABOUT 3 SHRIMP EACH

PER SERVING: 125 CALORIES, 1 G CARBOHYDRATE (0 G FIBER, 0 G ADDED SUGARS, 1 G NET CARBS), 15 G PROTEIN, 7 G FAT, 216 MG SODIUM.

TUNA WITH CANNELLINI BEANS, SPINACH, AND GARLIC

I make this for dinner when I have nothing planned and few groceries in the house. But I always seem to have these ingredients in my pantry and I'm always glad I made it!

2 tablespoons (30 ml) extra-virgin olive oil

1 cup (160 g) diced yellow or white onion

3 cloves garlic, smashed with wide side of knife

8 cups (240 g) packed baby spinach (or 5-ounce [140 g] package)

1 can (15.5-ounce [441 g]) cannellini beans, rinsed and drained

1 (5-ounce [140 g]) can tuna, drained

Zest of 1 lemon

1 teaspoon dried basil or Italian seasoning

¼ cup (60 ml) vegetable broth

1 tablespoon (15 ml) lemon juice

Heat a skillet over medium heat and add the oil. When the oil is hot, add the onion and garlic and cook for a few minutes, reducing the heat to medium-low as needed.

Reduce the heat to low and add the spinach, wilting it for a couple of minutes and stirring and flipping it a few times.

Add the beans, tuna, zest, and basil. Pour in the vegetable broth and lemon juice and heat through.

‹30 **TOTAL PREP AND COOK TIME: 30 MINUTES · YIELD: 3 SERVINGS, 1 ½ CUPS (325 G) EACH**

PER SERVING: 314 CALORIES, 35 G CARBOHYDRATE (9 G FIBER, 0 G ADDED SUGARS, 26 G NET CARBS), 23 G PROTEIN, 10 G FAT, 637 MG SODIUM

5

Savory Chicken, Beef, Pork, and Lamb

Get ready to shake things up with your protein staples, because I have a lot of new flavor combinations here for you.

GRILLED CHICKEN QUARTERS WITH OREGANO AND LEMON

Bone-in, skin-on chicken quarters, made of the thigh and leg, are among one of my favorite classic Sunday dinners. The skin becomes browned and crackly. When grilling chicken such as this, aim to keep the heat of the grill moderate so you don't burn the skin before the chicken cooks through.

You can either cook the chicken right away, or for a more intense lemony taste, marinate it for a few hours.

1 pound (455 g) chicken quarters (or thighs and drumsticks), trimmed

1 lemon, zest finely grated, plus 2 tablespoons (30 ml) juice

1 tablespoon (15 ml) extra-virgin olive oil

1 teaspoon dried oregano

1 clove garlic, smashed with wide side of knife

¼ teaspoon salt

Freshly ground black pepper

Cut the quarters through the joint, dividing the thigh from the leg. Place the chicken in a dish and cover with the lemon zest and juice, oil, oregano, garlic, salt, and pepper.

When ready to cook the chicken, preheat a grill to 375° to 400°F (190° to 200°C). Place the chicken on the grill, skin-side down, and cook until the skin is browned and the chicken is cooked nearly halfway through, about 10 minutes. Turn the chicken and cook through, about 5 minutes, or until an internal temperature thermometer reads 165°F (73°C). Remove and allow the chicken to rest for about 5 minutes before cutting.

Make It for the Whole Family
After rubbing the chicken with the oil, I just sprinkle salt on a portion for my kids.

 TOTAL PREP AND COOK TIME: 30 MINUTES · YIELD: 4 SERVINGS, 1 LEG OR 1 THIGH

PER SERVING: 161 CALORIES, 1 G CARBOHYDRATE (0 G FIBER, 0 G ADDED SUGARS, 1 G NET CARBS), 18 G PROTEIN, 9 G FAT, 222 MG SODIUM.

BAKED CHICKEN WITH NUTTY DUKKAH CRUST

Dukkah, pronounced DOO-kah, is a seasoning blend originating in Egypt. I created the recipe to yield a couple extra tablespoons of seasoning to reserve for other recipes, because once you taste this, I know you'll want to sprinkle it on everything from dips to snacks to fish to side dishes.

¼ cup (31 g) shelled, roasted pistachios

2 tablespoons (18 g) toasted sesame seeds

1 ¼ teaspoons (2 g) coriander seeds

½ teaspoon black peppercorns

1 ½ teaspoons ground cumin

½ teaspoon salt

1 ¼ pounds (568 g) chicken thighs or breasts, pounded to ½ inch (1.3 cm) thick, cut into 5 servings

1 tablespoon (15 ml) extra-virgin olive oil

Preheat the oven to 400°F (200°C, or gas mark 6) convection. Line a baking sheet with parchment paper.

Place the pistachios, sesame seeds, coriander, and peppercorns into a small food processor or personal-size blender. Process the ingredients until the pistachios are ground into small pieces, but not to a paste, a few seconds. Stir in the ground cumin and salt. Reserve 2 tablespoons (16 g) seasoning in a sealed container for use at a later time.

Coat the chicken completely in the remaining ground seasoning blend. Lay the chicken on the prepared baking sheet* and drizzle with the olive oil. Bake until cooked through, about 12 minutes.

Suggestions and Variations

Traditional dukkah also contains hazelnuts. If you happen to have some on hand, feel free to use half pistachios, half hazelnuts in this recipe.

Recipe Note

Alternatively, you may cook the seasoned chicken on the stovetop: Heat a sauté pan over medium heat. Add the oil and when it is hot, add the chicken and cook about halfway through on the first side, but before the seasonings burn, about 3 minutes. Turn and cook through, about 3 minutes.

Make It for the Whole Family

If you think your kids will hesitate trying the chicken with the dukkah seasoning, do what I do: reserve a piece of chicken and cut into nuggets. Sprinkle with salt and drizzle with olive oil, baking it on the same baking sheet, but in a different section, about 10 minutes.

TOTAL PREP AND COOK TIME: 30 MINUTES · YIELD: 5 SERVINGS

PER SERVING: 204 CALORIES, 3 G CARBOHYDRATE (1 G FIBER, 0 G ADDED SUGARS, 2 G NET CARBS), 27 G PROTEIN, 9 G FAT, 270 MG SODIUM.

Clean Eating Kitchen: The Low-Carb Mediterranean Cookbook

ROASTED CHICKEN WITH HERBES DE PROVENCE AND LEMON

Use fresh, not frozen, chicken for this when you can, which will yield juicier results. We love this chicken dish for Sunday dinners.

3 pounds (1365 g) chicken parts, skin on (like 2 breasts, 2 thighs, and 2 legs)

1 lemon, zest finely grated, then fruit cut in half

1 or 2 cloves garlic, thinly sliced

1 tablespoon (15 ml) extra-virgin olive oil

1 teaspoon kosher salt

2 tablespoons (11 g) dried herbes de Provence

Preheat the oven to 375°F (190°C, or gas mark 5). Line a baking sheet with parchment paper.

Pat the chicken dry. Slide the lemon zest and garlic under the skin of the chicken. Place the chicken on the prepared baking sheet, drizzle with the oil, and sprinkle with the salt and herbes de Provence. Roast for 25 to 30 minutes, until the edges are sizzling and cooked through. Allow the chicken to rest for 5 minutes before cutting. Spritz with half of the lemon.

TOTAL PREP AND COOK TIME: 45 MINUTES · YIELD: 6 SERVINGS, 1 PIECE EACH, SIZE VARIES

PER SERVING: 306 CALORIES, 0 G CARBOHYDRATE (0 G FIBER, 0 G ADDED SUGARS, 0 G NET CARBS), 33 G PROTEIN, 19 G FAT, 389 MG SODIUM.

CHICKEN GYRO LETTUCE WRAPS

I love gyros. So why not create a version that we can make at home with chicken? Marinate the chicken overnight for the full-flavor effect.

FOR THE CHICKEN:

1 ½ pound (683 g) boneless, skinless chicken breasts or breast fillets

1 lemon, zest finely grated, plus 2 tablespoons (30 ml) juice

1 clove garlic, sliced

½ teaspoon ground cumin

½ teaspoon dried oregano

½ teaspoon dried thyme

½ teaspoon salt

Freshly ground black pepper

FOR THE SANDWICH:

8 outer leaves iceberg lettuce

1 tomato, sliced

Very thinly sliced red onion

4 thin dill pickle spears

Tahini Sauce (page 118) or Cucumber Yogurt Salad (page 44)

To make the chicken: Place the chicken on a cutting board and cover with plastic wrap or parchment paper. Pound to ¼ inch (6 mm) thick and cut into 6 pieces. Combine the rest of the chicken ingredients in a wide, shallow dish, making the marinade. Coat the chicken in the marinade. Cover and refrigerate for at least 30 minutes, up to overnight.

When ready to cook the chicken, move the oven rack to 6 inches (15 cm) below the broiler element. Preheat the oven to low broil. Place the chicken on a baking sheet or broiler pan. When the broiler is ready, place the chicken in the oven on the top rack. Broil until the chicken is cooked through, about 7 minutes.

Tuck the chicken into the lettuce wraps and serve with the tomato slices, onion, pickles, and Tahini Sauce or Cucumber Yogurt Salad. Or both!

Suggestions and Variations
Gyros can also be made with lamb meat, like loin chops or rump.

TOTAL PREP AND COOK TIME: 30 MINUTES, PLUS MARINATING TIME · YIELD: 4 SERVINGS, 1 GYRO EACH

PER SERVING: 150 CALORIES, 3 G CARBOHYDRATE (1 G FIBER, 0 G ADDED SUGARS, 2 G NET CARBS), 26 G PROTEIN, 3 G FAT, 280 MG SODIUM.

BRAISED CHICKEN THIGHS WITH MUSHROOMS

While I know that many people prefer chicken breasts, personally, I'm a fan of thighs. I usually use skinless thighs in order to rein in the saturated fat, and I trim off any excess fat even further. As you simmer them, they become even more tender and juicy. Or feel free to leave the skin on, if you prefer (as pictured).

1 ¼ pounds (568 g) boneless, skinless chicken thighs, trimmed

½ teaspoon salt, divided

Freshly ground black pepper

1 tablespoon (15 ml) extra-virgin olive oil

1 package (8-ounce [225 g]) baby bella mushrooms, sliced

¼ medium onion, sliced ¼ inch (6 mm) thick

1 tablespoon (15 g) tomato paste

¼ cup (60 ml) dry red wine

1 cup (110 g) small red potatoes, quartered, then thinly sliced

¾ cup (175 ml) chicken bone broth

1 teaspoon herbes de Provence

Season the chicken with ¼ teaspoon of the salt and pepper. Heat a large skillet over medium-high heat. Add the oil. When the oil is shimmering, add the chicken. Brown on one side, about 7 minutes. Transfer to a plate.

Reduce the heat to low and add the mushrooms to the pan, browning them for about 10 minutes. About halfway through cooking the mushrooms, add the onion and cook until tender, about 5 minutes, scraping up the delicious brown bits from the bottom of the pan using a wooden spoon. Add the tomato paste to the pan *pincéing* it or "browning" it a bit, about 1 minute.

Pour in the wine, stir, and simmer to reduce the wine by half, a few minutes. Add the potatoes, broth and herbes de Provence and simmer to thicken the broth, about 10 minutes, until the potatoes are fork tender. Add the chicken back to the pan to finish cooking, a few minutes.

Nutrition Note
Living a low-carb lifestyle doesn't have to mean completely shunning the amazing potato if you keep the amount small and leave the skin on for added fiber.

TOTAL PREP AND COOK TIME: 30 MINUTES · YIELD: 4 SERVINGS, 1 THIGH WITH ½ CUP (70 G) VEGETABLES EACH

PER SERVING: 281 CALORIES, 13 G CARBOHYDRATE (2 G FIBER, 0 G ADDED SUGARS, 11 G NET CARBS), 28 G PROTEIN, 13 G FAT, 427 MG SODIUM.

SIMMERED TAHINI CHICKEN

This chicken dish, simmered in a creamy, nutty, lemony, sesame sauce, will kick you out of a food rut, for sure.

1¼ pounds (570 g) boneless, skinless chicken (thighs, breasts, or tenders), cut into at least 4 portions

¼ teaspoon salt

Freshly ground black pepper

1 tablespoon (15 ml) extra-virgin olive oil

¼ onion, thinly sliced

2 cloves garlic, minced

1 cup (235 ml) chicken bone broth

¼ cup (60 g) tahini

1 tablespoon (15 ml) lemon juice

1 tablespoon (15 ml) tamari or soy sauce

Plain Greek yogurt, for serving

Fresh herbs, like parsley, mint, or chives, coarsely chopped

Season the chicken with the salt and pepper. Heat a large skillet over medium heat. Add the oil to the pan. When the oil is shimmering, add the chicken. Brown on one side, 3 to 5 minutes. Turn and brown the other side. Transfer the chicken to a plate.

Add the onion and garlic to the pan, reducing heat as needed to medium-low, and cook until they become tender, about 5 minutes. Add the broth, tahini, lemon juice, and tamari, whisking the sauce until smooth and thickened, about 5 minutes. Spoon the sauce over the chicken and serve with a dollop of yogurt and a sprinkle of the fresh herbs.

TOTAL PREP AND COOK TIME: 30 MINUTES · YIELD: 4 SERVINGS

PER SERVING: 305 CALORIES, 4 G CARBOHYDRATE (1 G FIBER, 0 G ADDED SUGARS, 3 G NET CARBS), 27 G PROTEIN, 21 G FAT, 473 MG SODIUM.

MEDITERRANEAN MEATLOAF WITH ROASTED RED PEPPER SAUCE

I love a good meatloaf, and it can come in all sorts of delicious flavor combinations, shapes, and sizes. In this rendition, I go for a Spanish twist, with roasted red pepper sauce and smoked paprika, reminiscent of the Spanish meatballs *albondigas con tomate* you'll find in tapas taverns in Barcelona.

You can use jarred roasted red bell peppers or for something extra special, buy jarred piquillo peppers, which you can find in the international food section of well-stocked grocery stores.

Cooking oil spray

FOR THE MEATLOAF:

1 pound (455 g) lean ground beef or turkey

2 large eggs, beaten

¼ cup (24 g) almond flour

½ medium onion, grated or finely minced

2 teaspoons sweet or smoked paprika

1 clove garlic, minced, or 1 teaspoon garlic powder

2 teaspoons sherry vinegar or red wine vinegar

¼ teaspoon dried thyme

¼ teaspoon salt

Freshly ground black pepper

FOR THE SAUCE:

¾ cup (112 g) roasted red bell peppers or piquillo peppers

1 tablespoon (15 ml) extra-virgin olive oil

⅛ teaspoon salt

Preheat the oven to 375°F (190°C, or gas mark 5). Coat a bread pan with oil spray.

To make the meatloaf: Combine all of the meatloaf ingredients in a mixing bowl. Transfer to the pan and smooth out the top. Bake the meatloaf for 30 minutes. Top with the sauce and bake further to caramelize the top, about 15 minutes. Remove and allow to rest before slicing.

To make the sauce: Puree the sauce ingredients in a blender.

Make It for the Whole Family
- My kids only eat meatloaf, or "meatball cupcakes," as I call them, if it's baked in a muffin tin. Plus, I love it because they bake faster, in about 20 minutes.
- If you're not worried about a few more carbs, use dry rolled oats in place of almond flour.

Recipe Note
Piquillo peppers, a sweet, mild chile pepper, hail from northern Spain. They are roasted over embers, peeled, and then grilled and marinated, giving them an extra special taste.

TOTAL PREP AND COOK TIME: 1 HOUR · YIELD: 6 SERVINGS, 2 THIN SLICES EACH

PER SERVING: 229 CALORIES, 3 G CARBOHYDRATE (1 G FIBER, 0 G ADDED SUGARS, 2 G NET CARBS), 18 G PROTEIN, 16 G FAT, 220 MG SODIUM.

Savory Chicken, Beef, Pork, and Lamb

111

TURKEY SAUTÉ WITH RED BELL PEPPER

I made this up one day because I had some ground turkey in the fridge and I love hummus. It is packed with protein and vegetables, and you get to enjoy a hefty portion size and call it dinner. My husband simply raves about this dish. I love that it takes just 30 minutes to prepare from start to finish.

2 tablespoons (30 ml) extra-virgin olive oil, divided

1 pound (455 g) lean ground turkey

½ medium onion, diced (about 1 cup [160 g])

1 medium red bell pepper, diced (about 1 ½ cups [225 g])

1 or 2 cloves garlic, minced

½ teaspoon ground cinnamon

½ teaspoon ground cumin

1 lemon, zest finely grated, plus 1 tablespoon (15 ml) juice, divided

¼ cup (60 ml) chicken bone broth (or use regular broth)

2 tablespoons (30 g) hummus or Tahini-Zucchini Dip (page 21), plus more for serving

¼ teaspoon salt

Freshly ground black pepper

Fresh herbs, such as mint or Italian flat-leaf parsley, coarsely chopped

Large lettuce leaves or low-carb crackers

Heat a large sauté pan over medium-high heat and add 1 tablespoon (15 ml) of the oil. Add the turkey in a single layer and cook undisturbed for about 5 minutes. Turn the meat, and using a flat-edged wooden spoon, break up the meat. Transfer the meat to a plate.

Add the remaining 1 tablespoon (15 ml) oil to the pan and place over medium-low heat. Add the onion, bell pepper, and garlic and sauté until tender, about 5 minutes. Add the cinnamon and cumin and toast until aromatic, about 30 seconds. Add the cooked turkey back to the pan. Add the lemon zest, broth, hummus, salt, and pepper and simmer for about 5 minutes to blend the flavors. Stir in the lemon juice and fresh herbs.

Serve the turkey and hummus in lettuce wraps or with crackers.

Suggestions and Variations
- Ground beef or lamb would also work deliciously with this dish in place of turkey.
- I also like to sprinkle pomegranate arils on this when they're in peak season in the fall.

TOTAL PREP AND COOK TIME: 30 MINUTES · YIELD: 4 SERVINGS, 1 CUP (250 G) EACH

PER SERVING: 280 CALORIES, 10 G CARBOHYDRATE (2 G FIBER, 0 G ADDED SUGARS, 8 G NET CARBS), 23 G PROTEIN, 17 G FAT, 251 MG SODIUM.

ROTISSERIE CHICKEN STEW WITH KALE

I love to rotate in a rotisserie chicken every once in a while for an easy-peasy, yummy dinner. And let's face it, as soon as you bring it home is the best time to eat it. This recipe gives you a tasty way to use up the leftover chicken the next day, since simmering in broth moistens it right back up.

1 tablespoon (15 ml) extra-virgin olive oil

1 bag (5-ounce [142 g]) chopped kale

1 medium carrot, thinly sliced

2 cloves garlic, smashed with wide side of knife

3 ½ cups (805 ml) chicken bone broth

½ teaspoon Italian seasoning

½ cooked rotisserie chicken, cut into parts

Freshly ground black pepper

Place a large pot over medium heat. Add the oil. When the oil is shimmering, add the kale, carrot, and garlic. Sauté until the kale is mostly wilted and tender, about 5 minutes. Add the broth and Italian seasoning and cook over medium-high heat to get things moving. As soon as it comes to a simmer, add the chicken parts and flavorful chicken juices from the bottom of the container. Simmer until heated through.

Recipe Note
This recipe calls for the regular-size rotisserie chicken in stores, not the super-size chickens. Please make adjustments, as needed.

TOTAL PREP AND COOK TIME: 25 MINUTES · YIELD: 6 SERVINGS, 1 CUP (240 G) EACH

PER SERVING: 111 CALORIES, 2 G CARBOHYDRATE (1 G FIBER, 0 G ADDED SUGARS, 1 G NET CARBS), 17 G PROTEIN, 4 G FAT, 207 MG SODIUM.

CHICKEN MEATBALLS WITH FRESH ORANGE JAM

If you love those sticky-sweet cocktail meatballs served at parties, these may satisfy your craving with a lot less sugar.

FOR THE MEATBALLS:

2 eggs

1 pound (455 g) lean ground chicken

½ cup (80 g) finely diced onion

½ cup (45 g) old-fashioned rolled oats

1 orange, zest finely grated

2 cloves garlic, finely minced

½ teaspoon dried mint

½ teaspoon ground cinnamon

½ teaspoon ground cumin

¼ teaspoon salt

Freshly ground black pepper

2 tablespoons (30 ml) extra-virgin
 olive oil, divided

FOR THE JAM:

2 medium oranges

½ cup (120 ml) chicken bone broth

½ teaspoon arrowroot powder

Pinch of salt and pepper

To make the meatballs: Beat the eggs in a large mixing bowl. Add the chicken, onion, oats, orange zest, garlic, mint, cinnamon, cumin, salt, and pepper, stirring just until combined. Add cold water to a bowl for your hands. Heat a large skillet over medium-low heat and add 1 tablespoon (15 ml) of the oil. Moisten your hands in cold water, shaping the meat into one-tablespoon (15 g) balls.

Place the meatballs into the hot oil, rinsing your hand as needed if they start sticking to the meat. Brown the meatballs on all sides, about 2 minutes per side. You will likely need to cook the meatballs in two batches, so as not to overcrowd the pan. When all sides are browned, transfer the meatballs to a plate. After the first batch, remove any bits that linger in the pan. Add the remaining 1 tablespoon (15 ml) oil and cook the remaining meatballs.

To make the jam: Zest one of the oranges with a fine grater. Cut ¼ inch (6 mm) off each end of the oranges. Quarter the oranges, removing the seeds and excess membranes, then cut crosswise into pieces.

Heat the pan over medium-low heat. Add the oranges and zest and scrape in the juices remaining on the cutting board using a rubber spatula. With a wooden spoon, scrape browned bits from the bottom of the pan. Mix the chicken broth and arrowroot in a measuring cup, then pour it into the pan. Add a small pinch each of salt and pepper. Gently simmer until the oranges soften and the liquid thickens a bit, about 5 minutes, removing additional seeds if you spot any. Add the cooked meatballs and stir gently.

TOTAL PREP AND COOK TIME: 55 MINUTES · YIELD: 6 SERVINGS, 4 MEATBALLS EACH WITH 2 TABLESPOONS (46 G) JAM

PER SERVING: 227 CALORIES, 13 G CARBOHYDRATE (2 G FIBER, 0 G ADDED SUGARS, 11 G NET CARBS), 16 G PROTEIN, 13 G FAT, 190 MG SODIUM.

SHEET PAN PORK TENDERLOIN WITH GRAPES, WALNUTS, AND BLUE CHEESE

A handful of grapes goes a long way in contributing juicy pops of flavor with no added sugar.

1¼ pounds (568 g) pork tenderloin, trimmed (see Recipe Note)

1 cup (150 g) red grapes

½ medium onion, cut into eighths, chunks kept intact

8 smallish cloves garlic, tips cut off

½ teaspoon salt

Freshly ground black pepper

Small handful fresh thyme sprigs

¼ cup (30 g) walnut halves

¼ cup (30 g) crumbled blue cheese

Recipe Note

For the *most* tender tenderloin, it's important to cut off the "silver skin," the connective tissue that runs along the top of the pork. Ask a butcher to do it. Or, using a sharp boning knife, slide the tip of the knife under the widest part of the silver skin and use your other hand to hold the end of the pork, gliding the knife *away* from your hand. Angle the blade up just slightly in order to minimize cutting off any meat. Turn the pork around and repeat to cut off the remaining silver skin.

Place one oven rack in the middle of the oven and another rack 6 inches (15 cm) from the broiler element. Preheat the oven to 425°F (220°C, or gas mark 7). Line a baking sheet with parchment paper.

Place the pork, grapes, onion chunks, and garlic on the prepared baking sheet; it's best to cluster each ingredient for easier removal in case one of them cooks faster than the other, depending on the size of the tenderloin. Sprinkle with the salt and pepper. Pull the thyme leaves off with smooth, loose-grabbing pulls down the stems and sprinkle all over. Leave a spot for the walnuts (but don't add yet) in another area, keeping them away from the other ingredients so the walnuts stay crunchy. Bake for 5 minutes.

Add the walnuts to the pan. Bake for 10 more minutes, until the pork is sizzling around the edges, is no longer squishy in the middle, and a meat thermometer inserted into the middle reaches 135°F (57°C), since it will continue to rise to 145°F (62°C) after removing it from the oven.

Remove the pan from the oven. Set the broiler on low. Sprinkle the blue cheese on the pork, grapes, and onion. Broil for 3 minutes on the top rack, until the blue cheese begins to turn golden around the edges, but before the walnuts burn.

TOTAL PREP AND COOK TIME: 40 MINUTES · YIELD: 4 SERVINGS

PER SERVING: 247 CALORIES, 13 G CARBOHYDRATE (1 G FIBER, 0 G ADDED SUGARS, 12 G NET CARBS), 27 G PROTEIN, 10 G FAT, 359 MG SODIUM.

PORK TENDERLOIN WITH TAHINI SAUCE

If you love pork tenderloin, this recipe will reinvigorate your taste buds. I highly encourage you to get familiar with this cut of pork, if you're not already, because it is lean, easy to cook, and tender. Pounding the pork makes it even more tender.

FOR THE PORK:

1 pork tenderloin (about 1 pound [455 g]), trimmed

1 large egg

¼ cup (24 g) almond flour

½ teaspoon salt

¼ teaspoon garlic powder

Freshly ground black pepper

2 tablespoons (30 ml) extra-virgin olive oil, divided

FOR THE TAHINI SAUCE:

¼ cup (60 g) tahini

¼ cup (60 ml) water

1 tablespoon (15 ml) lemon juice

¼ teaspoon garlic powder

Pinch of salt

Fresh herbs, like parsley or mint, chopped

To make the pork: Cut the pork tenderloin into 1-inch (2.5 cm) thick medallions. Pound it to ¼-inch (6 mm) thickness. Whisk the egg in a wide, shallow dish. Combine the almond flour, salt, garlic powder, and pepper in another wide, shallow dish.

Place a large skillet over medium heat. Add 1 tablespoon (15 ml) of the oil. Dip the pork pieces in the egg and then in the almond flour. Add to the hot oil in a single layer. Cook until golden, about 5 minutes. Turn and add the remaining 1 tablespoon (15 ml) oil and cook for 2 to 3 more minutes, until done.

To make the tahini sauce: Combine the tahini, water, lemon juice, garlic powder, and salt in a small bowl.

Serve the pork with the sauce. Sprinkle with the herbs.

TOTAL PREP AND COOK TIME: 30 MINUTES · YIELD: 4 SERVINGS

PER SERVING: 285 CALORIES, 5 G CARBOHYDRATE (1 G FIBER, 0 G ADDED SUGARS, 4 G NET CARBS), 21 G PROTEIN, 21 G FAT, 389 MG SODIUM.

BAKED EGGPLANT WITH GROUND BEEF AND PINE NUTS

Here's another recipe from my grandma Helen's Lebanese kitchen for eggplant lovers, especially. It's like a Lebanese eggplant lasagna!

Cooking oil spray

2 tablespoons (30 ml) extra-virgin olive oil

1 medium eggplant, sliced lengthwise ¼-inch (6 mm)

½ teaspoon salt, divided

Freshly ground black pepper

1 pound (455 g) lean ground beef

½ medium onion, diced

2 cloves garlic, minced

⅓ cup (45 g) pine nuts

1 can (14.5-ounce [411 g]) crushed or diced tomatoes

2 tablespoons (30 ml) lemon juice

1¼ teaspoons dried mint

Za'atar seasoning (optional)

Preheat the oven to 350°F (180°C, or gas mark 4). Coat a 9 × 9-inch (23 × 23 cm) baking dish with cooking oil spray.

Heat a large sauté pan over medium heat. Add 1 tablespoon (15 ml) of the oil to the pan. Sprinkle the eggplant with ¼ teaspoon of the salt and pepper. Brown the eggplant on one side, about 5 minutes. Turn and brown the other side, about 3 minutes, adding the remaining 1 tablespoon (15 ml) oil. Transfer to a plate.

Put the pan back on medium-high heat. Add the beef, onion, garlic, pine nuts, remaining ¼ teaspoon salt, and pepper to the pan, and cook until the onions are tender, about 5 minutes. Add the tomatoes, lemon juice, and mint to the pan and stir.

Line the bottom of the baking dish with a layer of eggplant. Spoon half of the meat to cover the eggplant. Lay down another layer of eggplant and cover with the remaining meat. Bake on the bottom rack until bubbling around the edges, about 30 minutes. Allow it to rest for at least 10 minutes before cutting. Slice into 8 pieces. Sprinkle with za'atar seasoning, if desired.

Suggestions and Variations

If you're looking for a saucy side to pair with this, opt for plain Greek yogurt, Cucumber Yogurt Salad on page 44, or Tahini Sauce on, opposite, page 118.

TOTAL PREP AND COOK TIME: 1 HOUR · YIELD: 8 SERVINGS, 1 SLICE EACH

PER SERVING: 190 CALORIES, 10 G CARBOHYDRATE (3 G FIBER, 0 G ADDED SUGARS, 7 G NET CARBS), 14 G PROTEIN, 11 G FAT, 268 MG SODIUM.

MOROCCAN-SPICED LAMB CHOPS WITH MINT

You may season the lamb right before cooking, or season it earlier in the day or the day before to absorb more flavor.

FOR THE LAMB:

1 teaspoon ground coriander

½ teaspoon ground cumin

½ teaspoon paprika

½ teaspoon granulated garlic

¼ teaspoon salt

Freshly ground black pepper

1 pound (455 g) lamb chops or loin chops, trimmed

1 tablespoon (15 ml) extra-virgin olive oil

FOR THE MINT SAUCE:

½ cup (15 g) fresh mint leaves, chopped

2 teaspoons vinegar, like rice, malt, or white distilled vinegar

1 teaspoon extra-virgin olive oil

Pinch of salt

To make the lamb: In a wide, shallow dish or plate, combine the coriander, cumin, paprika, garlic, salt, and pepper. Dip the top sides of the lamb into the seasoning, then the bottom, then the sides. If you have any unseasoned areas left on the lamb, sprinkle with additional salt and pepper. If you will be cooking the lamb within an hour or two, you may leave on the counter. Otherwise, refrigerate the lamb, pulling it from the refrigerator at least 30 minutes before cooking so that it cooks evenly.

When ready to cook the lamb, preheat the oven to 400°F (200°C, or gas mark 6).

Heat a large ovenproof sauté pan over medium heat. Add the 1 tablespoon (15 ml) oil. When the oil is shimmering, add the lamb, top-side down. Cook until browned, about 4 minutes. Turn and brown the other side, about 4 minutes. If the lamb can stand up on its edges, then brown each edge. Transfer the pan to the oven and cook until medium-rare, 10 to 15 minutes. The time needed may be longer or shorter depending on the size and thickness of the lamb. Remove from the oven and allow the lamb to rest for at least 5 minutes before cutting.

To make the mint sauce: Combine the mint, vinegar, 1 teaspoon oil, and salt in a small bowl. Serve the lamb with the mint sauce.

Suggestions and Variations
I also enjoy lamb with flaked black lava salt sprinkled on the cut pieces.

TOTAL PREP AND COOK TIME: 30 MINUTES · YIELD: 2 SERVINGS

PER SERVING: 361 CALORIES, 2 G CARBOHYDRATE (1 G FIBER, 0 G ADDED SUGARS, 1 G NET CARBS), 37 G PROTEIN, 23 G FAT, 389 MG SODIUM.

Clean Eating Kitchen: The Low-Carb Mediterranean Cookbook

CHICKEN PAPRIKASH WITH MUSHROOMS

While Hungary is landlocked, I had to include this recipe for a variety of reasons. First, it's ridiculously delicious. Hungary is next to Croatia, a Mediterranean country. Hungary's southernmost wine region has been dubbed "The Mediterranean of Hungary." My husband has Hungarian roots, making *my* last name Dudash, which is so Hungarian. I made a few Mediterranean modifications, added mushrooms to the dish, plus lightened the dish with a few other techniques.

6 chicken thighs, skin-on, bone-in (about 2 pounds [910 g])

½ teaspoon salt, divided

Freshly ground black pepper

1 teaspoon avocado oil

1 container (8-ounce [227 g]) cremini mushrooms (about 2 ½ cups [175 g]), thickly sliced

½ medium onion, finely diced

3 tablespoons (45 g) sweet paprika, plus more to taste

1 cup (235 ml) chicken bone broth

1 or 2 tomatoes, chopped

1 Hungarian wax pepper, sliced (or ½ red bell pepper, diced)

¼ cup (60 g) 2% Greek yogurt or sour cream, plus more for serving

1 tablespoon (8 g) arrowroot powder

Blot the chicken dry with a paper towel and sprinkle the skin with ¼ teaspoon of the salt and pepper. Place a large sauté pan or skillet (I love to use my big cast-iron skillet for this) over medium-high heat and add the oil. When the oil is hot, add the chicken, skin-side down, and press gently on the centers with tongs. Brown for about 8 minutes, tilting the pan occasionally to redistribute the fat under the chicken and facilitate browning. Turn the chicken and move it to one side of the pan.

Add the mushrooms and sauté, scraping the brown bits from the bottom of the pan with a wooden spoon as the liquid releases. After a few minutes, add the onion and cook until translucent, about 5 minutes, reducing the heat to medium-low. Sprinkle the paprika and the remaining ¼ teaspoon salt over the mushrooms and stir.

Add the broth, tomatoes, and wax pepper. Cover loosely and simmer until the chicken is cooked through, about 20 minutes, reducing the heat to low as needed.

In a small bowl, combine the yogurt and arrowroot. Stir it into the sauce, keeping on the heat for 1 minute to thicken. Serve the chicken with the sauce, letting diners add more yogurt if desired.

TOTAL PREP AND COOK TIME: 1 HOUR · YIELD: 6 SERVINGS, 1 THIGH EACH WITH SAUCE AND VEGETABLES

PER SERVING: 345 CALORIES, 8 G CARBOHYDRATE (2 G FIBER, 0 G ADDED SUGARS, 6 G NET CARBS), 32 G PROTEIN, 21 G FAT, 342 MG SODIUM.

5-INGREDIENT CHICKEN TURMERIC BURGERS

Five simple pantry ingredients join forces to create a phenomenal taste with great depth. These burgers taste delicious served in lettuce wraps with a drizzle of liquid aminos, a dab of mayo, or Sriracha chili sauce, as my husband likes to smear on.

1 pound (455 g) ground chicken

¼ cup (40 g) finely chopped onion

1 clove garlic, minced

1 teaspoon ground ginger

½ teaspoon ground turmeric or curry powder

¼ teaspoon salt

Freshly ground black pepper

1 tablespoon + 1 teaspoon (20 ml) extra-virgin olive oil, divided

In a bowl, combine the chicken, onion, garlic, ginger, turmeric, salt, and pepper, using your hands or wooden spoon to distribute the seasonings evenly. Heat a large sauté pan, skillet, or griddle over medium heat. Add 1 tablespoon (15 ml) of the oil. Using a ¼-cup (60 g) measuring cup, scoop the chicken into the pan, molding each into thin patties, about 3 inches (7.5 cm) wide. You should get 8 patties. Brown on one side, about 3 minutes. Flip and brown the other side, about 2 minutes. If you still have chicken left to cook, scrape any bits from the pan. Place the pan back on the heat and add the remaining 1 teaspoon (5 ml) oil. Cook the remaining patties.

Recipe Note

Turmeric is a single-ingredient spice, contrary to curry powder, a seasoning blend that uses turmeric as a main ingredient. I recommend keeping a small bottle of turmeric on hand for use in chicken salad, simmering curry dishes, and stirring into turmeric lattes.

TOTAL PREP AND COOK TIME: 20 MINUTES · YIELD: 4 SERVINGS, 2 PATTIES EACH

<30

PER SERVING: 206 CALORIES, 1 G CARBOHYDRATE (0 G FIBER, 0 G ADDED SUGARS, 1 G NET CARBS), 20 G PROTEIN, 14 G FAT, 213 MG SODIUM.

SUMMER SQUASH STUFFED WITH BEEF WITH TOMATO SAUCE

My *Sithoo* made this dish of *koosa mehshee*, or stuffed summer squash, regularly. Except she used the Lebanese squash called koosa, which is pale green, faintly striped, and plumper on one end. Koosa isn't something you'll find in most stores (you may have luck at the farmers' market or Middle Eastern markets), so you can substitute with the thickest summer squash available, for easier stuffing.

My *Sithoo* used white rice in her recipe, but for this dish I swapped it out with quinoa, which is higher in protein and fiber.

8 medium summer squash,
   at least 1 to 1½ inches (2.5 to
   3.7 cm) in diameter

¼ teaspoon salt, plus for the squash

½ pound (227 g) lean ground beef

¼ cup (23 g) dry quinoa,
   rinsed using fine strainer

½ teaspoon dried dill or mint

⅛ teaspoon ground cinnamon

Freshly ground black pepper

1 tablespoon (15 ml) extra-virgin
   olive oil

1 clove garlic, minced

1 can (14.5-ounce [400 g])
   stewed tomatoes

Cut the stem ends off of the squash and just a thin slice off the other ends. Hollow out the squash using a zucchini corer or knife, reserving about half of the squash "guts," as my *Sithoo* called them. Poke a knife into the bottom of the squash to create an air gap. Sprinkle the insides of the hollowed-out squash with a bit of salt.

In a medium bowl, using a fork, gently combine the beef, quinoa, ¼ teaspoon salt, dill, cinnamon, and pepper. Stuff the squash with the beef, leaving ½ inch (1.3 cm) from the tops, allowing room for the quinoa to swell.

Put a large pot over medium heat and add the oil. When the oil is shimmering, add the garlic and squash "guts" and cook until softened, about 5 minutes. Pour in the tomatoes. Stand the squash up in the pot, open ends pointing up. Cover with a lid or foil. Simmer over medium-low heat until the meat is cooked through and the quinoa is tender, about 30 minutes, reducing the heat as needed. Serve with sauce spooned over the squash.

Recipe Note

If you don't have a zucchini corer, use a grapefruit knife or steak knife.

TOTAL PREP AND COOK TIME: 1 HOUR · YIELD: 8 SERVINGS, 1 SQUASH EACH

PER SERVING: 343 CALORIES, 26 G CARBOHYDRATE (4 G FIBER, 0 G ADDED SUGARS, 22 G NET CARBS), 26 G PROTEIN, 16 G FAT, 944 MG SODIUM.

BEEF STEW WITH MUSHROOMS AND RED WINE

The depth of flavor in this stew! It's total comfort food. Savoring this dish takes me back to a lovely meal enjoyed in the streets of Paris, on our way walking to Champs-Élysées. Not exactly Mediterranean, but oh-so-French and European.

1 tablespoon (15 ml) extra-virgin olive oil

1 pound (455 g) beef stew meat, cut into bite-size pieces

1 package (8-ounce [227 g]) baby bella mushrooms, quartered

3 tablespoons (48 g) tomato paste

½ cup (120 ml) dry red wine

3 ½ cups (823 ml) beef broth, divided

1 ¼ cups (137 g) diced red potatoes (2 medium red potatoes)

½ medium onion, diced (about 1 cup [160 g])

1 medium carrot, sliced into half-moons

2 cloves garlic

1 teaspoon herbes de Provence (or use Italian seasoning)

¼ teaspoon salt

Freshly ground black pepper

1 teaspoon arrowroot

Heat a soup pot over medium-high heat. Add the oil. When the oil is shimmering, add the meat and brown undisturbed for about 5 minutes. Stir and push the meat to the side of the pan. Add the mushrooms and brown, about 5 minutes. Stir in the tomato paste and brown it for a bit, about 1 minute. Pour in the wine. Using a wooden spoon, scrape the browned bits from the bottom of the pan, cooking the wine until nearly evaporated, a few minutes. Pour in 3 ¼ cups (765 ml) of the broth.

Add the potatoes, onion, carrot, garlic, herbes de Provence, salt, and pepper. Simmer until the beef and vegetables are tender, about 25 minutes. Dissolve the arrowroot in the remaining ¼ cup (60 ml) broth and pour into the stew. Stir and simmer for 5 minutes.

Suggestions and Variations
For another layer of color, texture, and flavor, garnish with fresh chopped chives.

Clean Eating Kitchen: The Low-Carb Mediterranean Cookbook

TOTAL PREP AND COOK TIME: 1½ HOURS · YIELD: 4 SERVINGS, 1 CUP (240 G) EACH

PER SERVING: 270 CALORIES, 20 G CARBOHYDRATE (3 G FIBER, 0 G ADDED SUGARS, 17 G NET CARBS), 25 G PROTEIN, 8 G FAT, 713 MG SODIUM.

BAKED LEBANESE MEAT KEBABS IN TOMATO SAUCE (*KAFTA*)

This is my sister Lauren's favorite weeknight dish and her whole family loves it. She is an awesome cook, always experimenting with all sorts of Mediterranean recipes. If you love lamb, you can go that route. If you're looking for a leaner option, she recommends using bison, or you can also use lean ground beef.

Cooking oil spray

¼ cup (34 g) pine nuts (or used slivered almonds)

¼ cup (42 g) dry quinoa

1 can (28-ounce [822 g]) fire-roasted diced or crushed tomatoes

½ teaspoon salt, plus more as needed

1 pound (455 g) ground lamb or bison

¼ medium onion, minced

1 tablespoon (15 ml) + 1 teaspoon lemon juice

2 cloves garlic, minced

1 teaspoon ground cumin

1 teaspoon dried mint

½ teaspoon ground coriander or garam masala, or use both

Freshly ground black pepper

¼ cup (15 g) Italian flat-leaf parsley leaves, coarsely chopped

Preheat the oven to 350°F (180°C, or gas mark 4). Coat a 9 × 13-inch (23 × 33 cm) baking dish with cooking oil spray.

Toast the pine nuts in a dry pan over low heat until golden, about 5 minutes. Soak the quinoa in ¼ cup (60 ml) water while you prep the other ingredients. Spread the tomatoes out in the prepared baking dish and sprinkle with a pinch of salt.

Combine the meat, onion, lemon juice, garlic, cumin, mint, coriander, salt, and pepper in a mixing bowl. Add the quinoa to the bowl, along with the cooled pine nuts. Shape into 12 meatballs. Flatten them slightly. Bake until the patties are cooked about halfway through, about 15 minutes. Turn the patties and bake until cooked through, about 10 minutes. Sprinkle with parsley.

Suggestions and Variations
If you have ground cardamom on hand, add ¼ teaspoon of that, too.

TOTAL PREP AND COOK TIME: 1 HOUR · YIELD: 4 SERVINGS, 3 PATTIES EACH, WITH SAUCE

PER SERVING: 333 CALORIES, 15 G CARBOHYDRATE (2 G FIBER, 0 G ADDED SUGARS, 13 G NET CARBS), 16 G PROTEIN, 24 G FAT, 458 MG SODIUM.

SHEET PAN CHICKEN WITH BELL PEPPERS AND PECANS

I love the ease of sheet pan dinners, where you place the protein and vegetables on one pan with the seasonings and cook it at the same time. This recipe is a go-to in our house.

2 pounds (910 g) chicken legs (about 6)

1 medium red bell pepper, cored and diced ¼-inch (6 mm)

1 medium green bell pepper, cored and diced ¼-inch (6 mm)

½ medium onion, diced (about 1 cup [160 g])

4 cloves garlic

2 tablespoons (30 ml) extra-virgin olive oil

1 teaspoon dried thyme

1 teaspoon dried basil

½ teaspoon salt

Freshly ground black pepper

½ cup (56 g) pecan halves

2 tablespoons (30 ml) balsamic vinegar

Preheat the oven to 400°F (200°C, or gas mark 6) convection. Line a large baking sheet with a silicone mat or parchment paper.

Place the chicken in a single layer on one side of the prepared pan and the peppers, onion, and garlic on the other side of the pan. Drizzle the oil and sprinkle the thyme, basil, salt, and pepper all over. Place the pecans in one section of the pan. Bake until the chicken is browned and cooked through, about 30 minutes. Remove from the oven and drizzle the vinegar on the chicken, peppers, and onions. Transfer chicken to a plate and stir the vegetables and pecans. Roast the vegetables a few minutes longer if they need it to become fork tender.

Suggestions and Variations

Feel free to swap the bell pepper with diced carrots, Brussels sprouts, or other vegetables you may have on hand. Just try to keep the amount the same.

Make It for the Whole Family

My kids love eating chicken legs, but they don't care for the sight of the mystery "green things" on it, so I skip the herbs on theirs and just season with salt. Everybody's happy!

TOTAL PREP AND COOK TIME: 1 HOUR · YIELD: 4 SERVINGS, ABOUT 2 LEGS EACH WITH ½ CUP (115 G) VEGETABLES

PER SERVING: 391 CALORIES, 11 G CARBOHYDRATE (3 G FIBER, 0 G ADDED SUGARS, 8 G NET CARBS), 27 G PROTEIN, 28 G FAT, 428 MG SODIUM.

STUFFED CABBAGE ROLLS WITH QUINOA AND CAULIFLOWER "RICE"

My grandma Helen's recipe, called *malfouf* in Lebanese, is a wonderful, baked dish packed with vegetables and protein. I took a few liberties with her recipe (naturally!), replacing rice with quinoa and cauliflower "rice." My husband doesn't even like cauliflower, and still loved this dish, since the cauliflower blends right in.

I like to roll these nice and plump, which means less rolling, for a time saver.

1 medium head green cabbage, core carved out from center

Kosher salt

1 pound (455 g) ground lamb or beef

2 cups (214 g) raw cauliflower rice*

1½ cups (270 g) canned diced tomatoes, divided

¼ cup (43 g) dry quinoa

½ teaspoon ground allspice (or use ¼ teaspoon cinnamon and ⅛ teaspoon nutmeg)

¼ teaspoon salt

Freshly ground black pepper

3 garlic cloves, smashed with side of wide knife

¼ cup (60 ml) + 1 tablespoon (15 ml) lemon juice (about 2 medium lemons)

Preheat oven to 350°F (180°C, or gas mark 4).

Fill a big pot with water and bring to a boil on high heat. Add the whole head of cabbage and boil for a few minutes until the leaves are softened. If the cabbage isn't completely covered, cover loosely with a lid, turning the cabbage after a minute. Do not over-cook or the leaves will tear while rolling. Using tongs, loosen each leaf and remove, transferring to a dish to cool. Trim and reserve the heavy center stems from the leaves, chopping up the scraps.

Make the stuffing by combining the lamb, cauliflower, ½ cup tomatoes, quinoa, allspice, salt, and pepper.

Roll about ¼ cup, slightly rounded, of the stuffing into each cabbage leaf, placing the stuffing crosswise at the base of the leaf. Roll it up like a burrito, tucking in the sides about halfway through rolling. Lay the rolls in a 13 × 9-inch (23 cm × 33 cm) baking dish, seam sides down. Sprinkle the remaining 1 cup (180 g) tomatoes, chopped cauliflower scraps, and smashed garlic over the rolls. Cover with foil and bake 45 minutes. Add the lemon juice and bake 10 more minutes.

Recipe Note
*Cauliflower "rice" is finely chopped cauliflower, mimicking the shape and size of rice, but without the carbs. You can now find it already chopped in the bagged salad section in well-stocked grocery stores.

TOTAL PREP AND COOK TIME: 1½ HOURS · YIELD: 6 SERVINGS, 2 ROLLS EACH

PER SERVING: 216 CALORIES, 17 G CARBOHYDRATE (5 G FIBER, 0 G ADDED SUGARS, 12 G NET CARBS), 16 G PROTEIN, 10 G FAT, 428 MG SODIUM.

6 *Vibrant Vegetable Sides*

Vegetables can be as gorgeous as any other course. I'm not shy about drizzling on good extra-virgin olive oil after cooking vegetables, either. Select vegetables according to their peak season near you whenever possible for the best texture, taste, price, and nutritional profile. Not to mention, it's better for the environment and your community.

ROASTED BRUSSELS SPROUTS WITH HERBES DE PROVENCE

If your only memories of Brussels sprouts are the boiled ones you grew up with, please allow me to help you make new memories. Crispy Brussels sprouts on restaurant menus are all the rage. You can easily make them at home, too, but without the bacon fat. During prime Brussels sprouts season (fall and winter), I cook these nearly once a week and my husband and I devour them.

1 pound (455 g) Brussels sprouts, washed, stems cut off, outer leaves peeled if needed, then quartered

2 tablespoons (30 ml) extra-virgin olive oil

½ teaspoon herbes de Provence (or Italian seasoning)

¼ teaspoon garlic powder

¼ teaspoon salt

Freshly ground black pepper

Preheat the oven to 425°F (220°C, or gas mark 7) convection. Line a baking sheet with parchment paper.

Place the Brussels sprouts on the prepared baking sheet and drizzle with the olive oil. Toss using tongs. Sprinkle with the herb seasoning, garlic powder, salt, and pepper. Roast until some of the leaves and bottoms become browned and crispy, about 10 minutes. Remove from the oven and stir. Roast until tender and most of the sprouts' outer leaves are browned and crispy.

Recipe Note

My favorite way to buy Brussels sprouts is while they are still on the stalk, which you can find at farmers' markets and some higher-end grocery stores. At the stores, look for nice and green, plump (not browned) outer leaves.

 TOTAL PREP AND COOK TIME: 30 MINUTES · YIELD: 4 SERVINGS

PER SERVING: 98 CALORIES, 8 G CARBOHYDRATE (3 G FIBER, 0 G ADDED SUGARS, 5 G NET CARBS), 3 G PROTEIN, 7 G FAT, 167 MG SODIUM.

UMAMI ROASTED PEPPERS WITH CRISPY POTATOES

If you're in a flavor rut with your veggies, this dish is for you. I love the brininess that the olives and capers add, plus the umami taste. Just embrace it. Trust me. If you decide to skip the olives and capers, I recommend spritzing with some lemon juice or balsamic vinegar after roasting the vegetables, to balance the flavor.

2 medium bell peppers (red, green, or yellow), cut into bite-size pieces

3 or 4 small red potatoes (about ½ pound [225 g]), thinly sliced

¼ medium red onion, diced

¼ cup (25 g) kalamata olives, sliced or filleted

3 cloves garlic, with skin on

1 teaspoon capers

2 tablespoons (30 ml) extra-virgin olive oil

½ teaspoon dried thyme

¼ teaspoon dried basil

¼ teaspoon salt, plus an extra pinch

Freshly ground black pepper

Preheat the oven to 350°F (180°C, or gas mark 4). Line a baking sheet with parchment paper or a silicone baking mat.

Place the peppers in one section of the prepared baking sheet. Arrange the potatoes in a single layer in another section, overlapping them a bit, and place the onion in another section. Sprinkle the peppers with the olives, garlic, and capers. Drizzle the oil on all of the vegetables, and sprinkle the thyme, basil, salt, and pepper all over. Bake until the potatoes are golden and the peppers tender, about 30 minutes.

Stir together the peppers and onions. Lay the potatoes alongside so you can enjoy their delightful crispiness.

Recipe Note

I use whatever small potatoes I have on hand for this recipe, like baby reds, purple, or gold.

Nutrition Note

Yup, I'm dishing up potatoes in a low-carb cookbook! Because life it too short to go without *any* heavenly, crispy potatoes. Instead of just a big pile of potatoes, I'm balancing them out with peppers and onions. Potatoes with the skins on contain more fiber, too.

TOTAL PREP AND COOK TIME: 1 HOUR · YIELD: 4 SERVINGS, ½ CUP (80 G) EACH

PER SERVING: 145 CALORIES, 18 G CARBOHYDRATE (3 G FIBER, 0 G ADDED SUGARS, 15 G NET CARBS), 2 G PROTEIN, 8 G FAT, 273 MG SODIUM.

WISPY PAN-FRIED ZUCCHINI

My husband and I enrolled in a cooking class at farm/restaurant Fattoria Terranova, just outside of Sorrento, Italy, a substantial town with breathtaking views of the Amalfi Coast. We loved the simplicity of their garden-fresh zucchini, thinly sliced and lightly fried in olive oil.

Extra-virgin olive oil, for frying

4 smallish zucchini, thinly sliced

¼ teaspoon salt

1 tablespoon (15 ml) white wine vinegar

¼ cup (7 g) coarsely chopped fresh mint

Line a large plate or platter with a few layers of paper towel.

Pour the olive oil into a skillet pan until it is about ¼ inch (6 mm) deep. Heat the oil over medium heat for a few minutes. Do not let it get to the smoke point. When the oil begins to shimmer, you can test it by adding a zucchini slice; it should immediately start bubbling around the edges. When the oil is the right temperature, add the zucchini to the pan. You may need to cook it in batches. Cook until it becomes golden on one side, then turn, about 5 minutes total. Lift the zucchini using a spider skimmer, fish spatula, or slotted spoon. Sprinkle with vinegar and mint.

TOTAL PREP AND COOK TIME: 20 MINUTES · YIELD: 4 SERVINGS, ½ CUP (125 G) EACH

PER SERVING: 83 CALORIES, 4 G CARBOHYDRATE (1 G FIBER, 0 G ADDED SUGARS, 3 G NET CARBS), 2 G PROTEIN, 7 G FAT, 156 MG SODIUM.

BAKED EGGPLANT AND PEPPERS WITH GARLIC

I love the mellow, earthiness of eggplant. It's like a sponge, soaking up whatever flavors you pair with it.

1 medium eggplant, cut into bite-size cubes

1 medium red or green bell pepper, cut into bite-size pieces

2 cloves garlic, minced

2 tablespoons (30 ml) extra-virgin olive oil, plus more for drizzling

¼ teaspoon salt

Pinch of crushed red pepper flakes

Freshly ground black pepper

Preheat the oven to 350°F (180°C, or gas mark 4).

Combine all of the ingredients in a 9 × 13-inch (23 × 33 cm) baking dish. Bake until the vegetables become tender, about 30 minutes. Drizzle with more oil for a richer taste.

TOTAL PREP AND COOK TIME: 45 MINUTES · YIELD: 6 SERVINGS, ½ CUP (133 G) EACH

PER SERVING: 60 CALORIES, 5 G CARBOHYDRATE (2 G FIBER, 0 G ADDED SUGARS, 3 G NET CARBS), 1 G PROTEIN, 5 G FAT, 99 MG SODIUM.

SAUTÉED RAINBOW SWISS CHARD

Rainbow Swiss chard is a nice way to mix things up in the greens department. It's a little heartier than other greens like spinach, but still tender.

1 bunch (11 ounces [310 g])
  Swiss chard

1 tablespoon (15 ml) extra-virgin
  olive oil

1 clove garlic, minced

Pinch of crushed red pepper flakes

1 teaspoon red wine vinegar

⅛ teaspoon salt

Freshly ground black pepper

First, prep the chard: Using a sharp knife (I like to use my agile boning knife for this), cut the ribs (the firm, center vein) away from the leaves, reserving the stems. Cut off the bottom ¼ inch (6 mm) of the ribs. Cut the ribs into manageable 4-inch (10 cm) or so pieces. Cut each piece lengthwise into equal-size strips. Then dice. Tear the leaves into smaller pieces.

Heat a large sauté pan* over medium heat. Add the oil. When the oil is shimmering, add the diced ribs, garlic, and red pepper flakes. Cook until tender, about 5 minutes. Add the leaves and cook until wilted and tender, about 5 minutes, reducing the heat as needed. Add the red wine vinegar, salt, and pepper and stir to combine.

Recipe Note

If you happened to sear meat with this meal, cook the chard in the same pan with the browned bits in the bottom of pan for added flavor.

TOTAL PREP AND COOK TIME: 20 MINUTES · YIELD: 4 SERVINGS, ½ CUP (87 G) EACH

<30

PER SERVING: 46 CALORIES, 3 G CARBOHYDRATE (1 G FIBER, 0 G ADDED SUGARS, 2 G NET CARBS), 1 G PROTEIN, 4 G FAT, 238 MG SODIUM.

ROASTED BROCCOLI WITH SUMAC

While I love steamed, boiled, or microwaved broccoli, roasting broccoli takes it to a whole other level. With crispy, browned florets and stems, this broccoli is gobbled up straight from the baking sheet before I even serve it on the plate. Even the stems are so good in this, so you don't have any food waste. Keep the broccoli nice and long. Splitting them lengthwise once or twice helps cut down on cooking time. The key to the crispiness is to crank your oven high enough, and on the convection setting, if you have it.

1 pound (455 g) broccoli (1 medium head), cut into stalks, then split

2 tablespoons (30 ml) extra-virgin olive oil

¼ teaspoon garlic powder

¼ teaspoon salt

Freshly ground black pepper

1 teaspoon ground sumac (see Recipe Note)

Preheat the oven to 425ºF (220ºC, or gas mark 7) convection (if available). Line a baking sheet with parchment paper.

Place the broccoli on the prepared baking sheet and drizzle with the olive oil. Toss using tongs. Sprinkle with the garlic powder, salt, and pepper. Roast for 15 minutes, until sizzling and browned on the bottom. Remove from the oven and sprinkle with the sumac.

Recipe Note
If you don't have or can't find sumac, add lemon zest before cooking, and spritz on lemon juice after cooking. Or a lemon pepper seasoning can also do the trick.

TOTAL PREP AND COOK TIME: 20 MINUTES · YIELD: 4 SERVINGS

<30 PER SERVING: 99 CALORIES, 7 G CARBOHYDRATE (3 G FIBER, 0 G ADDED SUGARS, 4 G NET CARBS), 3 G PROTEIN, 7 G FAT, 183 MG SODIUM.

CAULIFLOWER "RICE" RISOTTO

In the beginning of my career, I cooked as a line chef at a Mobil 5-Star restaurant, Mary Elaine's, a modern French restaurant with Mediterranean influences. The risotto was absolutely addicting, just oozing with all of the good things, like mascarpone, Parmesan, and some fine dining unmentionables like bone marrow and loads of butter. A benefit of using cauliflower rice in place of actual Arborio rice is that it cooks much faster.

I like to top this with browned, sliced chicken sausage and call it a meal.

2 tablespoons (30 ml) extra-virgin olive oil, divided

1 container (8-ounce [227 g]) button mushrooms, quartered

2 fresh thyme sprigs (or ¼ teaspoon dried)

¼ teaspoon +⅛ teaspoon salt, divided

¼ cup (60 ml) dry white wine or dry vermouth

12 ounces (340 g) cauliflower "rice"

¼ medium white or yellow onion, minced (about ⅓ cup or 55 g)

¼ cup (60 ml) vegetable broth or chicken bone broth

¼ cup (60 g) mascarpone or cream cheese

½ cup (50 g) grated Parmesan cheese, plus extra for garnish

1 teaspoon sherry vinegar

Heat a large skillet over medium heat. Add 1 tablespoon (15 ml) of the oil. When the oil is shimmering, add the mushrooms, thyme, and ⅛ teaspoon of the salt. Brown for about 5 minutes. Remove the pan from the heat while you pour in the wine. Place it back on the heat and cook until the liquid evaporates quickly. Transfer the mushrooms to a plate and discard the thyme sprigs.

Put the pan back on the heat and add the remaining 1 tablespoon (15 ml) oil. Add the cauliflower and onion. Sauté until the vegetables become tender, about 5 minutes. Reduce the heat to low and add the broth, both cheeses, and remaining ¼ teaspoon salt. Stir and heat gently just enough to melt the cheese. Stir in the vinegar. Serve the cauliflower topped with the mushrooms.

TOTAL PREP AND COOK TIME: 30 MINUTES · YIELD: 4 SERVINGS, ⅔ CUP (200 G) EACH

<30

PER SERVING: 213 CALORIES, 9 G CARBOHYDRATE (2 G FIBER, 0 G ADDED SUGARS, 7 G NET CARBS), 7 G PROTEIN, 16 G FAT, 469 MG SODIUM.

BAKED STUFFED ARTICHOKE

While I enjoy canned or jarred artichokes as super quick toppers, fresh artichokes provide an elevated taste and textural experience. It's really just the artichoke heart that is worth eating—which is at the core of this plant and also runs down the center of the stem.

There are two ways to get to the creamy core. One way is a bit laborious, accomplished by cutting away all of the leaves and peeling the stem. I do this on occasion and did it often during my fine dining line cook days.

The method used in this recipe is easier. You just stuff the goodies into the center and bake the entire artichoke, and eat it by placing a leaf between your teeth, pulling off the creamy center. As a kid, I always looked forward to it. My mom used bread crumbs, but in this version I swapped them out with almond flour.

1 large artichoke

2 tablespoons (12 g) unpacked almond flour

2 tablespoons (10 g) grated Parmesan cheese

2 tablespoons (30 ml) lemon juice, divided

1 clove garlic, minced

¼ teaspoon salt

Freshly ground black pepper

2 tablespoons (30 ml) extra-virgin olive oil

Preheat the oven to 350°F (180°C, or gas mark 4).

Cut the very tips of the artichoke leaves with kitchen shears about ½ inch (12 mm) from the top. Trim a slice off from the stem. Quarter the artichoke lengthwise. Scoop out the "fur" with a spoon.

In a bowl, combine the almond flour, Parmesan, 1 tablespoon (15 ml) of the lemon juice, garlic, salt, and pepper. Place the artichoke in a baking dish, cut-side up. Stuff the filling into the scooped-out core and drizzle with olive oil. Cover and bake until the artichoke is fork tender in the middle, about 20 minutes. Drizzle with the remaining 1 tablespoon (15 ml) lemon juice.

To serve, pull off leaves of the artichoke, pulling the leaf through your teeth. Also don't miss out on the creamy center core.

TOTAL PREP AND COOK TIME: 45 MINUTES · YIELD: 4 SERVINGS, ¼ ARTICHOKE EACH

PER SERVING: 112 CALORIES, 6 G CARBOHYDRATE (2 G FIBER, 0 G ADDED SUGARS, 4 G NET CARBS), 2 G PROTEIN, 9 G FAT, 211 MG SODIUM.

PESTO ZOODLES

You haven't truly lived until you've made and tasted homemade pesto. I made my version without Parmesan, but you can certainly sprinkle it over the dish at the end, as I did in this recipe. These zoodles are so satisfying and beautifully accent light seafood and chicken dishes. I spritz in the lemon juice right before eating to preserve the bright green color.

FOR THE PESTO:

1 clove garlic, peeled

¼ cup (34 g) pine nuts or walnuts

2 cups (80 g) fresh basil leaves

¼ teaspoon kosher salt

¼ cup (60 ml) extra-virgin olive oil

FOR THE ZOODLES:

1 tablespoon (15 ml) extra-virgin olive oil

2 cloves garlic, with skin on

1 pound (455 g) zucchini, spiralized, then cut into manageable lengths

¼ teaspoon salt

Freshly ground black pepper

1 ½ teaspoons lemon juice

Grated Parmesan cheese, for serving

To make the pesto: Place the garlic and nuts in a food processor and blend until minced. Add the basil and salt and blend to a paste. Drizzle in the oil and blend until incorporated.

To make the zoodles: Heat a large sauté pan over medium-low heat and add the oil. When the oil is shimmering, add the garlic and sauté until aromatic, about 1 minute. Add the zoodles and sauté until they're nearly tender enough to twirl around a fork like spaghetti and are bright green, about 5 minutes. Remove the garlic. Sprinkle with the salt and pepper toward the end of cooking.

Combine the pesto and the zoodles. Spritz the zoodles with the lemon juice right before eating. Sprinkle the Parmesan over the zoodles.

TOTAL PREP AND COOK TIME: 30 MINUTES · YIELD: 4 SERVINGS, ½ CUP (112 G) EACH

PER SERVING: 235 CALORIES, 6 G CARBOHYDRATE (2 G FIBER, 0 G ADDED SUGARS, 4 G NET CARBS), 3 G PROTEIN, 23 G FAT, 302 MG SODIUM.

ANYTIME ROASTED VEGETABLES WITH HERBES DE PROVENCE

This is a good standby vegetable recipe, since these vegetables are widely available year-round in good condition and pair well with pretty much any main dish you're preparing. These vegetables cut into smaller pieces cook up quickly, too.

3 portobello mushrooms, stems snapped off, gills scooped out, and caps sliced

1 cup (150 g) cherry tomatoes, halved

¼ red onion, thinly sliced

1 medium zucchini, sliced

3 tablespoons (45 ml) extra-virgin olive oil, divided

1 teaspoon herbes de Provence (or Italian seasoning)

¼ teaspoon salt

Freshly ground black pepper

1 ½ teaspoons balsamic vinegar

Preheat the oven to 350°F (180°C, or gas mark 4). Line a baking sheet with parchment paper or a silicone baking mat.

Place the vegetables on the prepared baking sheet in a single layer. Drizzle with 2 tablespoons (30 ml) of the oil and sprinkle with the herbs, salt, and pepper. Roast until the vegetables are tender, 20 to 25 minutes. Drizzle with the balsamic vinegar and the remaining 1 tablespoon (15 ml) oil.

TOTAL PREP AND COOK TIME: 30 MINUTES · YIELD: 4 SERVINGS, ½ CUP (45 G) EACH

<30 PER SERVING: 124 CALORIES, 7 G CARBOHYDRATE (2 G FIBER, 0 G ADDED SUGARS, 5 G NET CARBS), 2 G PROTEIN, 11 G FAT, 160 MG SODIUM.

ROASTED SPAGHETTI SQUASH AND TOMATOES

Part "pasta," part vegetable, 100 percent delicious. Roasted spaghetti squash makes for a delicious side dish or base for chicken, Bolognese sauce, and more.

1 small spaghetti squash
(1½ to 2 pounds [680 to 910 g])

2 tablespoons (30 ml) extra-virgin olive oil, divided

¼ teaspoon salt, divided, plus more to taste

Freshly ground black pepper

1 cup (150 g) cherry tomatoes, halved

¼ teaspoon dried thyme

¼ cup (10 g) fresh basil leaves, hand-tear the larger ones

Preheat the oven to 375°F (180°C, or gas mark 4). Line a baking sheet with a silicone baking mat or parchment paper.

Slice off the top and bottom ¼ inch (6 mm) of the squash. Cut the squash in half lengthwise and scoop out the seeds. Drizzle with 1 tablespoon (15 ml) of the oil and season with ⅛ teaspoon of the salt and some pepper. Place the squash on one side of the prepared baking sheet, cut-side down.

On a piece of foil, about 10 × 10 inches (25 × 25 cm), spread the tomatoes in a single layer and top with 2 teaspoons (10 ml) of the oil, the thyme, the remaining ⅛ teaspoon salt, and pepper. Fold all sides of the foil straight up to create an edge, keeping the juices and oil inside as it bakes. Move the foil boat to the pan.

Bake the squash and tomatoes until tender and softened, about 30 minutes. Carefully remove the foil boat from the pan. Continue to bake the squash until it is sizzling around the edges and a fork pierces very easily through the skin, about 10 minutes more.

Carefully turn the squash over to release the steam. When it is cool enough to handle, shred the squash with a fork to create strands. When the fork is no longer pulling up strands, you can use a spoon to scrape the remaining squash from the skin.

To serve, place the squash in a shallow bowl or platter. Sprinkle the tomatoes on top, drizzle with the remaining 1 teaspoon (5 ml) oil, fresh basil leaves, and salt and pepper to taste.

TOTAL PREP AND COOK TIME: 60 MINUTES · YIELD: 4 SERVINGS, 1 CUP (155 G) EACH

PER SERVING: 130 CALORIES, 16 G CARBOHYDRATE (4 G FIBER, 0 G ADDED SUGARS, 12 G NET CARBS), 2 G PROTEIN, 8 G FAT, 182 MG SODIUM.

ROASTED CAULIFLOWER WITH CASHEWS AND TURMERIC

It is surprising how satisfying and filling this cauliflower can be! I tend to gobble this up while preparing the rest of dinner.

1 small head cauliflower, cut into bite-size florets (about 6 cups, or 600 g)

1 teaspoon ground turmeric

½ teaspoon garlic powder

½ teaspoon ground cumin

¼ teaspoon salt

Freshly ground black pepper

2 tablespoons (30 ml) extra-virgin olive oil

¼ cup (32 g) roasted cashews, chopped through twice (or use slivered or sliced almonds)

Preheat the oven to 425°F (220°C, or gas mark 7) convection. Line a baking sheet with parchment paper or a silicone baking mat.

Place the cauliflower on the prepared baking sheet. In a small bowl, combine the turmeric, garlic powder, cumin, salt, and pepper. Drizzle the cauliflower with the oil. Sprinkle with the seasonings. Sprinkle on the cashews. Roast until the cauliflower is fork tender, about 15 minutes.

<30

TOTAL PREP AND COOK TIME: 30 MINUTES · YIELD: 4 SERVINGS, 1 CUP (270 G) EACH

PER SERVING: 150 CALORIES, 11 G CARBOHYDRATE (3 G FIBER, 0 G ADDED SUGARS, 8 G NET CARBS), 4 G PROTEIN, 11 G FAT, 193 MG SODIUM.

ROASTED BUTTERNUT SQUASH WITH CELERY AND PEPITAS

When fall arrives, I get so excited seeing winter squash displays at grocery stores and farmers' markets. Here is one more way you can enjoy them.

1 small butternut squash
(about 1½ pounds [680 g])

2 tablespoons (30 ml) extra-virgin
olive oil

½ teaspoon ground cumin

½ teaspoon ground coriander

¼ teaspoon salt

Freshly ground black pepper

3 stalks celery, diced into
bite-sized pieces

¼ cup (30 g) toasted pepitas
(pumpkin seeds)

Juice from ½ of an orange

Preheat the oven to 450°F (230°C, or gas mark 8) convection. Line a large baking sheet with parchment paper.

Poke the squash all over with a fork and micro-wave for 2 minutes for easier peeling. Cut off the stem and cut the squash in half lengthwise. Peel off the skin and scoop out the seeds and stringy pulp. Cut the squash into bite-size pieces and place on the pre-pared baking sheet. Drizzle with the oil and sprinkle with the cumin, coriander, salt, and pepper. Toss with a spatula to coat evenly. Bake for 15 minutes. Remove from the oven and add the celery. Bake until the vegetables are caramelized and fork-tender, 15 to 20 minutes, sprinkling in the pepitas during the last 5 minutes of baking. Squeeze on orange juice.

TOTAL PREP AND COOK TIME: 1 HOUR · YIELD: 8 SERVINGS, ½ CUP (70 G) EACH

PER SERVING: 135 CALORIES, 8 G CARBOHYDRATE (2 G FIBER, 0 G ADDED SUGARS, 6 G NET CARBS), 5 G PROTEIN, 10 G FAT, 123 MG SODIUM.

7 La Dolce Vita: Sweets and Fruit Dishes

While I find that savory dishes really don't need added sugar at all, most desserts are another story. I'd rather have a few good bites of a really good and satisfying dessert than one made with noncaloric sweeteners. Therefore, you're going to see some added sugar in most of these desserts. I try to offset the sugar, however, with fiber-filled ingredients, like nuts and seeds, naturally sweet fruit, and whole grains. If you've experimented with noncaloric sweeteners before and enjoy them, then by all means, feel free to swap sweeteners in as you feel comfortable doing.

I also included some cheese and fruit-based recipes. In French cuisine, a cheese plate is traditionally served after dessert. It's a satisfying way to end a meal.

BURRATA CHEESE WITH BALSAMIC-MARINATED STRAWBERRIES

If you're a cheese lover, you will fully appreciate the extra creaminess of this Italian cheese, comprised of a mozzarella shell encasing oozy, thick cream. It has so many applications: as an appetizer, plopped on a salad, melted over pasta, and yes, as a final course. Because why not? But try to cut into only the amount of burrata you will use in one sitting, as you will lose the tender consistency over time once the package is open and cheese is cut.

In this recipe, I dress up the burrata with marinated strawberries. Make sure you're only using fragrant and sweet strawberries, trimming off any white shoulders.

1 cup (170 g) diced strawberries

1 tablespoon (15 ml) balsamic vinegar

2 teaspoons honey

¼ cup (36 g) sliced almonds

Fresh basil leaves

1 large (8-ounce [226 g]) ball burrata or 2 small (4-ounce [113 g]) balls

In a bowl, combine the strawberries, balsamic, and honey.

Toast the almonds in a dry sauté pan over medium-low heat, stirring frequently, a few minutes, reducing the heat to low as needed.

For the basil leaves, there are two different ways you can prepare them. Either snip the tiny leaves and use them whole. Or stack larger leaves, roll them the wide way, and thinly slice into ribbons using a sharp knife or kitchen shears.

When ready to serve, drain the burrata. If serving buffet-style, leave the burrata whole and place it in the center of the platter. If plating individually, cut into portions. Spoon on the strawberries and juices. Sprinkle with the almonds and basil.

Make It for the Whole Family
Even my husband, who usually does not enjoy sweet mixed with savory, loved this dish. However, another substitute for people who like things more traditional is using ripe, quartered cherry tomatoes instead of strawberries. Omit the honey and sprinkle with sea salt.

TOTAL PREP AND COOK TIME: 30 MINUTES · YIELD: 4 SERVINGS

<30

PER SERVING: 221 CALORIES, 8 G CARBOHYDRATE (2 G FIBER, 3 G ADDED SUGARS, 6 G NET CARBS), 8 G PROTEIN, 18 G FAT, 77 MG SODIUM.

GOAT CHEESE TRUFFLES WITH PISTACHIOS AND FIGS

Goat cheese, pistachios, and figs—a perfect combination to turn into dessert. Figs contain no added sugar and a whopping 5 grams fiber per serving, whether they are fresh or dried. Serve with almond flour crackers or pair with sliced roasted chicken.

½ cup (56 g) finely chopped shelled pistachios

½ cup (75 g) dried figs, finely chopped

1 package (4-ounce [115 g]) soft fresh goat cheese

¼ cup (120 g) mascarpone or cream cheese

2 teaspoons lemon juice

⅛ teaspoon ground nutmeg

⅛ teaspoon salt

Freshly ground black pepper

Honey, for drizzling (optional)

Place the pistachios and figs in a wide, shallow dish.

In a bowl with an electric mixer, whip the goat cheese and mascarpone until smooth, a few minutes. (Or, if you soften the cheeses at room temperature first, you can mix it by hand.) Add the lemon juice, nutmeg, salt, and pepper, and whip until incorporated.

Use your hands to roll the cheese into bite-size balls. Then roll them in the pistachios and figs. Drop a bit of honey on each truffle, if desired, for added effect.

Suggestions and Variations
You can swap the pistachios out for toasted walnuts, pine nuts, pecans, or almonds.

TOTAL PREP AND COOK TIME: 30 MINUTES · YIELD: 6 SERVINGS

PER SERVING: 172 CALORIES, 11 G CARBOHYDRATE (2 G FIBER, 0 G ADDED SUGARS, 9 G NET CARBS), 7 G PROTEIN, 12 G FAT, 167 MG SODIUM.

CHOCOLATE ALMOND FLOUR CAKE WITH ORANGE

This moist, soft chocolate cake is flourless and grain-free, made of almond flour. I like to eat it plain, like a snack cake, or dollop on whipped cream.

1 cup (175 g) dark or semisweet chocolate chips

½ cup (115 g) unsalted butter, sliced or softened

¾ cup (150 g) sugar, divided

1 teaspoon almond or vanilla extract

6 large eggs, yolks and whites separated, at room temperature

1 ½ cups (144 g) almond flour (not packed)

Zest of 1 lemon

Zest of 1 orange

Pinch of salt

Whipped cream, for serving (optional)

Make It for the Whole Family
You may want to remove the orange and lemon zests for your kids' sake, since the citrus may seem bitter to them. If you'd like to enjoy the cake for yourself and other adults, then carry on with your bad self.

Preheat the oven to 350°F (180°C, or gas mark 4). Butter a 9-inch (23 cm) springform pan. Line the inside base with parchment paper. Butter the paper.

Place the chocolate chips in a bowl and microwave for 1 minute. Stir well. Microwave for another 15 to 30 seconds and stir until the chocolate is smooth.

In a large bowl of an electric mixer with the paddle attachment, beat the butter, ½ cup (100 g) of the sugar, and the almond extract on high speed until very light and fluffy, about 5 minutes. Add the egg yolks one at a time, completely incorporating after each addition. Stir in the almond flour, melted chocolate, and citrus zests.

In a second clean mixing bowl, beat the egg whites with the salt on low speed until foamy. Increase the speed to high and beat in the remaining ¼ cup (50 g) sugar. Beat until the whites hold soft peaks (the tips will slump over a bit when you lift the whisk from the eggs).

Fold a fourth of the whites into the chocolate mixture. Gently fold in the remaining whites. Scoop the batter into the prepared pan. Bake until the cake is set around the edges but still soft and moist in the center, about 38 minutes. Cool for 10 minutes.

Invert the cake onto a cooling rack and peel off the paper. You can invert it again so that the crusty side is facing up. Cool completely. Serve with whipped cream, if desired.

TOTAL PREP AND COOK TIME: 1 HOUR · YIELD: 16 SERVINGS, 1 SLICE EACH

PER SERVING: 226 CALORIES, 18 G CARBOHYDRATE (2 G FIBER, 9 G ADDED SUGARS, 16 G NET CARBS), 5 G PROTEIN, 16 G FAT, 64 MG SODIUM.

BERRY TART WITH MASCARPONE CREAM AND ALMOND FLOUR CRUST

I love the simple ingredients in this fresh dessert that is flourless and contains very little added sugar, yet is totally satisfying. If you're not familiar with mascarpone cheese, you've probably enjoyed it and didn't realize it, since it's the creamy filling found in the Italian dessert tiramisu. It has the texture of cream cheese but with a comforting mellow taste, rather than tangy.

FOR THE CRUST:

Cooking oil spray

1¼ cups (150 g) almond flour or meal

3 tablespoons (42 ml) unsalted butter, melted

1 tablespoon (21 g) honey

¼ teaspoon ground cinnamon

⅛ teaspoon salt

¼ cup (43 g) dark or semisweet chocolate chips

FOR THE MASCARPONE FILLING:

1 container (8-ounce [226 g]) mascarpone cheese, softened at room temperature for 30 minutes

2 tablespoons (30 ml) amaretto liqueur

1½ cups (240 g) fresh fruit, like raspberries, blueberries and sliced strawberries and figs

To make the crust: Preheat the oven to 350ºF (180ºC, or gas mark 4). Coat three 4½ × 4½-inch (11.4 × 11.4 cm) tartlet pans* with cooking oil spray.

Combine the almond flour, melted butter, honey, cinnamon, and salt in a bowl. Press into the bottom and lower half of the sides of the prepared pans. Bake until golden and the edges pull away slightly from the sides, 12 to 13 minutes. Let cool in the pans.

Remove the cooled crusts from the pans. Microwave the chocolate in a bowl in 30-second increments, stirring in between, for a total of about 1½ minutes. Stir until smooth. Drizzle the chocolate in the crusts and spread to completely cover the bottom and lower half of the sides.

To make the filling: In a bowl with an electric mixer, whip the mascarpone on high speed until smooth, about 1 minute. Add the amaretto and whip to incorporate.

Spread the cream over the set chocolate crusts. Arrange the fruit on top.

Make It for the Whole Family
You may prefer to use 2 teaspoons vanilla or almond extract plus a drizzle of honey in place of the amaretto liqueur.

Suggestions and Variations
* If you have mini tartlet pans or one large tart pan, by all means, feel free to use them. You will need to adjust the baking time, since smaller pans will take less time and larger pans will take more time.

TOTAL PREP AND COOK TIME: 45 MINUTES, PLUS COOLING TIME · YIELD: 6 SERVINGS, ½ TART EACH

PER SERVING: 405 CALORIES, 19 G CARBOHYDRATE (4 G FIBER, 3 G ADDED SUGARS, 15 G NET CARBS), 8 G PROTEIN, 34 G FAT, 70 MG SODIUM.

CRISPY OVEN-DRIED ORANGE SLICES

I am obsessed with these wispy things with a concentrated, intense orange flavor. The first time I tried them was as a drink garnish, but I saved it before it fell into the drink, otherwise what a shame that would have been! Enjoy them as is for a sweet treat, or serve with cheese.

2 oranges

4 teaspoons (28 g) honey

⅛ teaspoon ground cinnamon

2 teaspoons warm water

Preheat the oven to 300°F (150°C, or gas mark 2). Line two baking sheets with parchment or a silicone baking mat.

Using a serrated knife, cut the oranges crosswise into ⅛-inch (3 mm) slices. You should get 8 slices per orange. Remove the seeds. Spread out the oranges on the prepared baking sheets. Combine the honey, cinnamon, and water in a small bowl, and brush this generously onto the oranges. Shake the pan gently back and forth to distribute the honey underneath the oranges. Bake until bubbling around the edges and appearing slightly dried out, about 30 minutes. Let cool. Store in an airtight container.

TOTAL PREP AND COOK TIME: 45 MINUTES · YIELD: 8 SERVINGS, 2 SLICES EACH

PER SERVING: 26 CALORIES, 7 G CARBOHYDRATE (1 G FIBER, 3 G ADDED SUGARS, 6 G NET CARBS), 0 G PROTEIN, 0 G FAT, 0 MG SODIUM.

CRUNCHY ALMOND CLUSTERS

These small but satisfying petits fours accompanied our daily morning espresso drinks while staying in Rovinj, Croatia, at Hotel Lone. I looked forward to them every morning.

2 egg whites

½ cup (100 g) sugar

½ teaspoon almond extract

3 cups (330 g) sliced almonds

Preheat the oven to 350°F (180°C, or gas mark 4). Line a baking sheet with parchment paper.

In a clean bowl, beat the egg whites and sugar with a mixer on high speed until soft peaks form. Add the almond extract and mix again quickly. Fold in the almonds.

Using a tablespoon (15 g) scoop, spoon the mixture onto the prepared baking sheet. You should get 32 cookies. Bake in batches until golden, about 12 minutes. Cool completely before storing in a sealed container.

TOTAL PREP AND COOK TIME: 30 MINUTES · YIELD: 32 SERVINGS, 1 EACH

<30 PER SERVING: 64 CALORIES, 5 G CARBOHYDRATE (1 G FIBER, 3 G ADDED SUGARS, 4 G NET CARBS), 2 G PROTEIN, 4 G FAT, 4 MG SODIUM.

EASY PEAR CRISP WITH ALMOND-WALNUT TOPPING

Since this fruity dish contains no added sugar, it can be enjoyed for breakfast, as a side dish anytime, with cheeses, or for dessert. If you'd like to make it more decadent, sprinkle in some of your preferred sweetener before baking it, drizzle on honey afterward, or dollop on a scoop of low-carb ice cream.

Cooking oil spray

FOR THE FILLING:

6 small pears, halved, cored, and sliced ¼ inch (6 mm) thick (about 4 ½ cups [540 g])

2 tablespoons (28 g) cold unsalted butter, thinly sliced

1 teaspoon lemon juice

1 teaspoon arrowroot powder

½ teaspoon ground coriander

½ teaspoon ground ginger

½ teaspoon ground cinnamon

Freshly ground black pepper

Pinch of salt

FOR THE TOPPING:

½ cup (55 g) sliced almonds

½ cup (60 g) walnuts, chopped

1 teaspoon chia seeds

Preheat the oven to 350°F (180°C, or gas mark 4). Coat a 9 × 9-inch (23 × 23 cm) baking pan with cooking oil spray.

To make the filling: Combine all of the filling ingredients in a bowl. Spread the pears in the prepared pan.

To make the topping: Combine the topping ingredients. Sprinkle over the pears in an even layer.

Bake until the almonds become golden and you can see or hear the pears sizzling around the edges, about 35 minutes. Allow the crisp to set for at least 10 minutes.

Nutrition Note

Pears contain a remarkably high amount of fiber, with 6 grams per medium pear, which equals 21 percent of the Recommended Daily Intake. The skin contains most of the fiber, so I urge you to leave it on; just give it a good rinse and pat dry.

TOTAL PREP AND COOK TIME: 55 MINUTES · YIELD: 12 SERVINGS

PER SERVING: 107 CALORIES, 10 G CARBOHYDRATE (3 G FIBER, 0 G ADDED SUGARS, 7 G NET CARBS), 2 G PROTEIN, 7 G FAT, 13 MG SODIUM.

GRILLED PEACHES WITH CINNAMON RICOTTA CRÈME

Once peach season hits in the summer, I cannot get enough. I eat them whole as is, chopped and sprinkled over yogurt or breakfast cereal, in cobblers, and yes, grilled. The direct heat of the grill caramelizes the natural sugars in the peaches. This is a super simple dessert you can whip up on a grill night or any night, and you don't even have to heat up the kitchen.

FOR THE RICOTTA:

1 cup (250 g) whole-milk
  ricotta cheese

2 teaspoons honey

⅛ teaspoon ground cinnamon

⅛ teaspoon ground nutmeg
  (or freshly grated)

FOR THE PEACHES:

2 ripe peaches

¼ cup (36 g) sliced almonds, toasted

Preheat the grill to just slightly above medium, about 400°F (200°C).

To make the ricotta: Stir together the ricotta ingredients.

To make the peaches: Cut the peaches in half, twisting them apart into two halves. If they are stubborn, use your paring knife to release. Pull or cut out the pits. Place the peaches, cut-side down, on the grill and cook undisturbed until they get nice grill marks, about 5 minutes. Turn the peaches and grill until the skins start to pull away, or you have a nice grill mark, 2 to 3 minutes.

Scoop a dollop of the ricotta into a dish, place a peach half on top, and sprinkle on the almonds.

<30 TOTAL PREP AND COOK TIME: 20 MINUTES · YIELD: 4 SERVINGS, ½ PEACH, WITH ¼ CUP (63 G) RICOTTA EACH

PER SERVING: 165 CALORIES, 16 G CARBOHYDRATE (2 G FIBER, 3 G ADDED SUGARS, 14 G NET CARBS), 7 G PROTEIN, 9 G FAT, 68 MG SODIUM.

GRILLED WATERMELON WITH GOAT CHEESE AND MINT

Watermelon is the ultimate thirst quencher and palate cleanser during the dead of summer. People are surprised to hear that 1 cup (150 g) of watermelon is only 11 grams carbs. Watermelon is largely comprised of—you guessed it—water.

¼ cup (60 ml) balsamic vinegar (see Recipe Note)

1 teaspoon honey

4 thick watermelon wedges, rind on

1 tablespoon (15 ml) extra-virgin olive oil

⅛ teaspoon salt

4 ounces (115 g) soft goat cheese

¼ cup (8 g) mint leaves, coarsely chopped

Preheat the grill to medium-high heat, about 400°F (200°C).

Pour the balsamic into a small saucepan and bring to a simmer over medium heat. Simmer until the balsamic reduces by about half, about 4 minutes. Remove from the heat and stir in the honey.

Brush the watermelon with the oil and sprinkle with the salt. Place the watermelon on the hot grill and cook until you see grill marks, about 5 minutes. Turn, and make grill marks on the other side, about 3 minutes. Remove and cut off the rind.

Place one piece of watermelon on a plate. Spread with some of the goat cheese, place another slice of watermelon on top, and spread with more goat cheese. Drizzle with the balsamic and sprinkle with the mint.

Recipe Note

I usually just have balsamic that has been aged for a number of months. If you have a pricier balsamic on hand that has been aged for years, by all means, use that and you won't need to reduce it or add honey because it will already be naturally thickened and mellow.

TOTAL PREP AND COOK TIME: 30 MINUTES · YIELD: 4 SERVINGS

<30 PER SERVING: 158 CALORIES, 12 G CARBOHYDRATE (1 G FIBER, 1 G ADDED SUGARS, 11 G NET CARBS), 6 G PROTEIN, 10 G FAT, 207 MG SODIUM.

MINI RICOTTA CHEESECAKES WITH WALNUT CRUST

Ricotta, an Italian cheese made from the whey left over from other cheeses, has a light texture but rich taste and isn't tangy like cream cheese. It's what is used in lasagna fillings, but when you puree it, like in this recipe, it's no longer grainy and becomes silky smooth.

You can make these cheesecakes with or without the crusts. Either way, you'll have a satisfying, creamy dessert.

Cooking oil spray

FOR THE CRUST:

1 cup (120 g) chopped walnuts

1 tablespoon (7 g) flaxseed meal

¼ teaspoon ground cinnamon

Pinch of salt

1 tablespoon (15 ml) water

1 teaspoon honey

FOR THE FILLING:

1 container (15-ounce [469 g]) ricotta cheese

⅓ cup (115 g) mild-flavored honey, like clover

3 large eggs

3 tablespoons (24 g) arrowroot powder

1 medium orange, zest finely grated, plus 1 tablespoon (15 ml) juice

1 small vanilla bean, cut in half lengthwise and seeds scraped out (or use 1½ teaspoons vanilla extract)

⅛ teaspoon salt

Fresh berries and shaved dark chocolate, for serving

Preheat the oven to 375°F (190°C, or gas mark 5). Coat 11 cups of a muffin tin with oil spray.

To make the crust: Add the walnuts, flaxseed, cinnamon, and a pinch of salt to a food processor. Pulse until the walnuts are finely chopped. Sprinkle in the water and honey, and pulse a few more seconds until the walnuts are fine crumbs but not nut butter. Press into the bottoms of the muffin tin cups. Bake for 10 to 11 minutes, until aromatic and golden.

Set the oven to 350°F (180°C, or gas mark 4) when the crusts are done baking.

To make the filling: Pour the liquid off of the ricotta and process in a food processor until smooth. Add the honey, eggs, arrowroot, orange zest and juice, vanilla seeds, and salt. Pour the ricotta into the muffin tins onto each crust, about ¼ cup (60 ml) each. Bake until the tops are firm in the middle, not wavy, and no longer soupy, 15 to 20 minutes.

Let cool to room temperature, then chill in the refrigerator. Run a knife tightly around the edges to release the cheesecakes. Use a tiny spatula or fork to carefully lift the cheesecakes out of the tins. Garnish with berries and shaved chocolate.

TOTAL PREP AND COOK TIME: 1 HOUR · YIELD: 11 SERVINGS, 1 CHEESECAKE EACH

PER SERVING: 184 CALORIES, 14 G CARBOHYDRATE (1 G FIBER, 9 G ADDED SUGARS, 13 G NET CARBS), 6 G PROTEIN, 12 G FAT, 101 MG SODIUM.

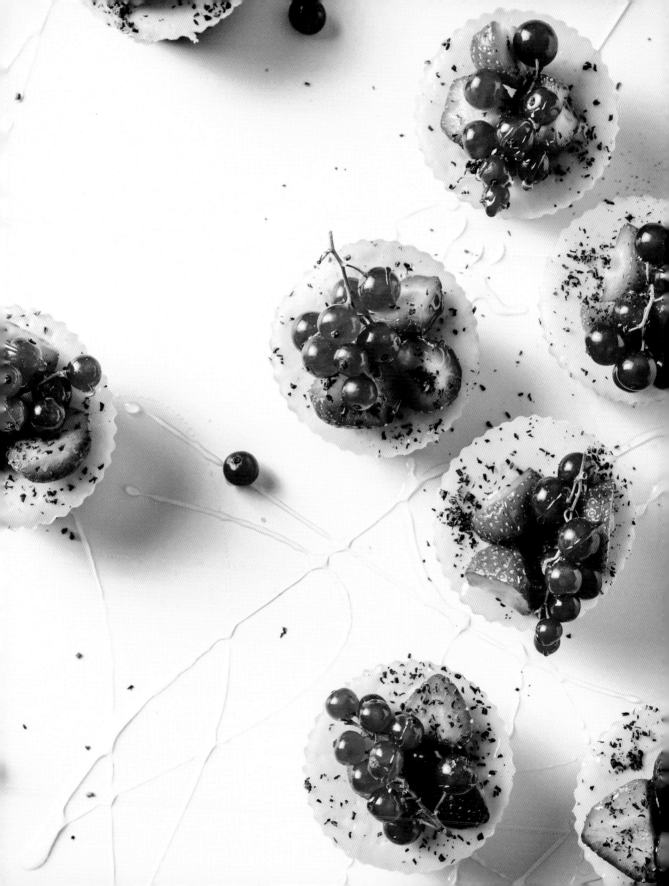

MINI MOLTEN CHOCOLATE CAKES

Back in my days working in a fine dining French restaurant with Mediterranean influences (R.I.P., Mary Elaine's), I recall the decadent lava cakes the pastry chefs made. Life-changing.

I changed things up in this rendition, replacing the wheat flour with coconut flour, which reduces the grams of carbs and increases the fiber.

The key to a gooey, oozing center is to not overcook the cakes, so I recommend keeping the oven light on and watching closely during the last few minutes of baking.

Cooking oil spray

½ cup (113 g) unsalted butter

4 ounces (113 g) 70% dark chocolate, chopped

4 large eggs

2 tablespoons (30 ml) brandy or cognac

⅓ cup (78 g) sugar

⅓ cup (37 g) coconut flour (see Recipe Note)

Fresh raspberries, for serving

Preheat the oven to 375°F (190°C, or gas mark 5) convection. Spray 6 ramekins with oil.

Microwave the butter and chocolate in a medium glass bowl for 30 seconds. Stir and microwave for 30 more seconds. Stir until smooth.

Stir in the eggs and brandy. Add the sugar and flour and whisk to combine. Divide the batter among the ramekins.

Bake until the top appears mostly dry, except in the middle it should look a little wet, 8 to 9 minutes. Remove from the oven.

Pick up a ramekin using an oven mitt or folded kitchen towel (the ramekins will be hot!) and place a plate on top of the ramekin. Turn your hands, inverting the ramekin to the top and the plate to the bottom. The cake should easily slide out. Garnish with raspberries.

Recipe Note
If you don't have coconut flour, you may substitute with wheat flour.

TOTAL PREP AND COOK TIME: 30 MINUTES · YIELD: 6 SERVINGS, 1 EACH

<30

PER SERVING: 367 CALORIES, 29 G CARBOHYDRATE (4 G FIBER, 15 G ADDED SUGARS, 25 G NET CARBS), 6 G PROTEIN, 25 G FAT, 54 MG SODIUM.

VEGAN CHOCOLATE MOUSSE WITH AQUAFABA

You will not believe your eyes as you watch aquafaba, the cooking liquid from chickpeas, whip up into a light, puffy cloud, taking the place of eggs in this mousse. When you are craving a deep, dark chocolaty taste that you can lick off a spoon, this dessert is it!

1 cup (175 g) dark or semisweet chocolate chips or chopped chocolate bar

2 tablespoons (26 g) sugar, divided

2 teaspoons milk

½ teaspoon almond or vanilla extract

Pinch of salt

½ cup (120 ml) aquafaba (the liquid from 1 can no-salt-added chickpeas), at room temperature

½ teaspoon cream of tartar

Toasted slivered almonds, for serving

Chopped fruit like strawberries, clementines, or raspberries, for serving

First, melt the chocolate. For this, you have two different options:

The "easy" way: Microwave the chocolate in a microwavable bowl for 1 minute. Stir. Microwave for 30 seconds. Stir. Microwave for 15 seconds and stir many times until smooth.

The purist way: Heat 1 inch (2.5 cm) of water in a saucepan over medium heat. Place the chocolate in a glass or metal bowl and place on top of the saucepan. Stir occasionally and reduce the heat as needed to maintain a simmer. Heat and stir until smooth.

To the melted chocolate, stir in 1 tablespoon (13 g) of the sugar, milk, almond extract, and salt. Transfer to a large mixing bowl.

In a separate bowl, whip the aquafaba in a stand mixer with the whisk attachment or use a handheld mixer. Beat on high speed until frothy, about 1 minute. Add the cream of tartar and mix until the aquafaba becomes fluffy. Add the remaining 1 tablespoon (13 g) sugar and beat until it reaches stiff peaks.

Fold one-fourth of the aquafaba into the chocolate until incorporated. Then fold in another big dollop. Continue a couple more times until all of the aquafaba is used up. Do not overmix or the mousse will lose its airiness. Portion into four serving dishes, like ramekins, martini glasses, or small bowls. Cover and chill for a few hours.

Garnish with the almonds and fruit.

Recipe Note

Portion into ¼ cup (45 g) shot glasses for extra portion control.

TOTAL PREP AND COOK TIME: 30 MINUTES, PLUS CHILLING TIME · YIELD: 4 SERVINGS, ½ CUP (90 G) EACH

PER SERVING: 240 CALORIES, 36 G CARBOHYDRATE (3 G FIBER, 6 G ADDED SUGARS, 30 G NET CARBS), 2 G PROTEIN, 13 G FAT, 45 MG SODIUM.

Resources

Dietary Carbohydrate Restriction as the First Approach in Diabetes Management. R. Feinman, W. Pogozelski, A. Astrup. *Nutrition*. Vol. 1, Issue 1, January 2015, pages 1–13. Accessed at https://www.sciencedirect.com/

FoodData Central. U.S. Department of Agriculture, Agricultural Research Service. https://fdc.nal.usda.gov.

"Macro- and Micronutrients in a Traditional Greek Menu." *Forum Nutrition*. 2005.

"Macronutrient and Major Food Group Intake in a Cohort of Southern Italian Adults." *Antioxidants*. 2018.

"Macronutrient Distribution and Dietary Sources in the Spanish Population: Findings from the ANIBES Study." Number 7. Spanish Nutrition Foundation. 2015.

Nutitionist Pro™ Nexgen Axxya Systems nutrient analysis database. 2020. https://www.nutritionistpro.com/

Oldways Culural Food Traditions. The Mediterranean Diet. https://oldwayspt.org/

U.S. Department of Health and Human Services and U.S. Department of Agriculture. *2015–2020 Dietary Guidelines for Americans*. 8th edition. December 2015.

Acknowledgments

While it is *such* a wonderful feeling to create and bring a new book into the world, it takes a whole team of support and talented experts specializing in different parts of the book process to make it a really special piece for the reader to experience.

This book all began with me emailing my idea in just a few sentences to my trusted editor, Amanda Waddell, at Fair Winds Press. Over the next few months, the idea grew into mini proposal and one day—boom—we received the greenlight to turn it into an actual book. Lydia Rasmussen slid in as interim editor during Amanda's maternity leave to help me massage some fine details.

While I created and tested the 100+ recipes, my trusted personal assistant Elizabeth Wells turned my "chicken scratch" recipe notes, measurements, and headnotes into precisely typed and coded recipes, allowing me to focus on the creative process while she mastered metric measurements and kept the kitchen in order. My Lebanese family, Jenn Wilke, Nancy Rahn, and Barb Richter, helped me source the original recipes of Grandma Helen and *Sithoo*—thank you for all of the back and forth.

The recipes then moved on to the talented art director Heather Godin and photographer Joanne Harding. Jo and I were up to the task of hunting down ingredients during the worldwide lockdown at the start of the pandemic. Mission accomplished.

On to the nutritional analyses—thank you, Tyler Florek, for jumping on board to calculate every last carb, calorie, and protein gram so I could focus on recipe testing.

When you commit to writing 40,000 words in four months, it's helpful to have cheerleaders on the sidelines, like my friends who sampled my many food creations, including Christin and Jack Barber. My registered dietitian colleagues who believe in me and my big ideas and serve as role models—you have no idea how much that means to me and how much you motivate me every single day: DJ Blatner, Janet Helm, Maggie Moon, Bonnie Taub-Dix, Ellie Krieger, Toby Amidor, Liz Weiss, Carolyn O'Neil, Sharon Palmer, Mitzi Dulan, Leslie Bonci, Rosanne Rust, Joy Bauer, and many more to name.

I cherish my media family who always welcomes me on to share recipe inspiration, including my friends at Indy Style, Arizona Midday, and Lori Corbin of ABC Los Angeles.

Thank you to my husband, Steve, for his undying support as I poured over the manuscript for hundreds of hours upon hours, giving me the time to write this book. His consolation prize was eating very well for months on end. And appreciation goes out to my sweet daughters, Scarlet and Stella, for being so patient when "Mommy's working" and providing candid recipe critiques, helping me shape motivating messages to parents trying to feed their families right while meeting their own personal goals.

To my readers, viewers, home cooks, and followers: You inspire me every day with your comments, questions, and feedback. I'm always listening to deliver to you what matters to *you* most.

About the Author

Michelle Dudash, R.D.N., is an award-winning registered dietitian nutritionist, Cordon Bleu-certified chef, founder of Dash Dinners™ Spice Kits, and a television personality. Her recipes and articles have appeared in *Food Network*, *Men's Journal*, *Diabetic Living*, *EatingWell*, *Shape*, *SELF*, and *Better Homes and Gardens*. She is frequently quoted in publications such as *O, The Oprah Magazine*, *Women's Health*, *The Washington Post*, *WebMD*, *Forbes*, *Today*, *Bon Appetit*, *Prevention*, *Family Circle*, *Woman's Day*, *Everyday Health*, and *Women's World* and has appeared nationally on *The Rachael Ray Show*, *The Doctors*, *The Chew*, *The List*, *FOX and Friends*, *Cheddar TV*, and *Cavuto*. She is the author of the cookbook *Clean Eating for Busy Families*, revised and expanded.

Michelle has cooked at a Mobil Five-Star restaurant and was a private chef, serving guests including English royalty. She graduated from the University of Wisconsin-Madison with a bachelor of science in dietetics, and a few years later she earned her toque from Le Cordon Bleu College of Culinary Arts in Scottsdale, Arizona. She lives in Carmel, Indiana, with her husband and two daughters.

Visit Michelle online at michelledudash.com or on social media.

Facebook:
Michelle Dudash, RD

Twitter, Instagram, and Pinterest:
@michelledudash

Index